Clarborough
and
Welham
from 1778

Kath Sutton

Every effort has been made to check the facts in this book, however, I acknowledge that readers may want to correct or add extra detail. I would be most grateful for such information, so that amendments may be noted.
Kath Sutton

First published 2015
Bookworm of Retford
1 Spa Lane, Retford Notts. DN22 6EA
www.bookwormretford.co.uk

ISBN 978-0992785727

The map on the cover has been reproduced by kind permission of
The Nottinghamshire Archives
Photos by John Sutton

Contents

Foreword

The idea of writing a book arose after four old books were rediscovered in the Clarborough and Welham Parish Council Office: one was a copy of the Inclosure Award 1778 and the others were three old Parish Council Minute books beginning in 1894. On reading these, some fascinating facts were discovered which caught my imagination, and I asked the Parish Councillors of 2014 if they were happy for me to write a book based on two of them. I am grateful that they gave their permission.

Kath Sutton

Parish Councillors 2014:
Chairman Phil Gibson
Vice-chairman Ann Codling
Barry Codling
Lesley Baines
Maurice Collins
Brian Grice
Brian Robinson
Freda Robinson

Standing left to right: Lesley Baines, Barry Codling,
Brian Robinson, Brian Grice.
Seated left to right:Vice -chairman Ann Codling,
Cairman Phil Gibson, Freda Robinson.
Maurice Collins was unavailable at the time of the photograph

(Photo by John Sutton)

Acknowledgements

This book has been a collaborative effort and would not have been possible without the help of many groups and individuals. I am greatly indebted to all those mentioned below.
First of all, I wish to thank the Sharing Heritage Initiative, which is a funding programme that helps people across the UK explore, conserve and share all aspects of the history and character of their local area. The Heritage Lottery Fund provided us with a grant that has made it possible to fund this book, without which it would simply have been a computerised copy lodged in the Parish Council Offices. It also funded the setting-up of our web page.

Secondly, I thank the members of the Clarborough and Welham Parish Council, who gave me permission to use the books rediscovered in the Parish Council Offices, and always gave me their unstinted support.
Thirdly, thanks are extended to all the villagers in Clarborough and Welham who willingly gave their time, and infused this project with enthusiasm, sweeping it forward.

Thank you to all the librarians at the Retford Reference Library who were most patient with my many queries, as were the staff at the Nottinghamshire Archives. The staff at the Bassetlaw Museum, thankfully shared our enthusiasm, particularly Helen. Mr. Richard Bunn, the Head teacher at Clarborough Village School, was most supportive and encouraged the pupils to participate. Paul and Angela from Bookworm were so helpful and integrated the photographs into the text; they also published the book. And finally John, who discussed this project with me endlessly and helpfully. He was also our photographer.
Thank you everyone,
Kath Sutton

Contributors
Chris Boothby
Helen Shaw Brown
Edna Bradley
Richard Bunn – Head teacher of Clarborough School
Rev. Mark Cantrill
Ann and Louis Cobb
Ann and Barry Codling
Thelma Cooke
Christine Durham
Sharon Davison
Janet Freeborough
John Goacher
Judith Gourlay
Rosetta Gleadon
Carolyn Halford
Ruth Hunter
Janet Hill
Sheila and Brian Hogg
Edith Jackson
Linda Lane
Joan and Verdon Marshall
Ray Pask
Parish Councillors of Clarborough and Welham
Pupils of Clarborough School
Freda and Brian Robinson
John Sutton
Barbara Swannack
Joan Tacy
Stella and Lewis Taylor
Marjorie Thornton
Glyn and Jenny Whelan
Jacque and Jeff Williamson

Introduction

After I had read the copy of the Inclosure Award 1778 and the three old Parish Council Minute books I was inevitably drawn into the life of the villages. I read of names and places, some old, some still a part of the village, which invited further investigation – so here it is.

The most enjoyable aspect of this study to me has been the reminiscences of the villagers who were able to take me into the past and relive some of the key points in their lives and that of the villages. I am so very grateful for their time, effort and enthusiasm, and truly hope that they enjoy reading this book.

I have, of course, only touched the surface. There is only so much that can be included and the sections have been carefully selected. Many more fascinating stories are there to be discovered, and maybe some of you might begin to delve more into your own personal family histories.

All I do know is that we are all so fortunate to be living in our attractive rural situation, with its kindly, hospitable and friendly people.

Chapter One

The Inclosure Award

On the inner cover of the Copy of Clareborough Inclosure Award 1778 is written the following:

'Award, consisting of 79 pages with map at the end. Copy of Clareborough Parish Council, received November 25, 1941 from N.C.C To be kept in the care of Ross M.Phillipson, Chairman of the Council Welham Yew Tree Dairy farm, near Retford. The original award of 1778 to be kept in the Muniment Room, Shire Hall, Nottingham for safe custody where it may be inspected by any parishioner or his solicitor on written application to the clerk, Notts County Council'.

Thus the book has been in the possession of Clarborough Parish Council now for over seventy years and has possibly not been read or studied by very many parishioners. It is a difficult book to read as there are no sentences as we know them, merely continuous prose separated by the occasional comma and many capital letters. Sadly, the copy of the map is not able to be reproduced but it is still in the Clarborough and Welham Parish Council Office where it may be viewed on request.

Before Enclosures

It would be useful to remind ourselves of the situation before Enclosures. It is well known that, except in one or two special areas, the farming of the country was carried on almost into modern times under the old methods associated with the famous Open Field System. This was where almost all the villagers had shares or strips in the three fields of the village, though by no means equal; this was governed through a committee of the most popular and respected members of the village. The three fields alternated their crops and one field was always kept fallow to regain its goodness. When enclosures came it affected the countryside in the same ways as the Industrial Revolution affected the towns.

It really arose because of the growing discontent of proprietors with the rigid Open Field System, which prevented them from modernising their methods of farming. When they decided to change over in our area it was heralded with many visits to where it had already happened, much discussion and worry about the cost which would be incurred, but hopes of what they would benefit from modernisation and the expected increase in productivity.

The petitioners for the Inclosure Act were John Hewitt Esq., Lord of the Manor of Oswaldbeck Soke, several proprietors, and other persons interested. The lands mentioned in the petition were open arable fields, meadows, stinted common pastures and free Commons. The Bill was to be prepared and brought in by Lord E. Bentinck and Lord G. Cavendish. The Clarborough and Welham Inclosure Act is listed under the heading that, along with other areas, the proprietors were not unanimous in desiring enclosure.

Three Commissioners were appointed to deal with the enclosures and what a difficult job this must have been, sorting out claims, values and conflicting interests! Whether it was these difficulties, or the age of the commissioners, one knows not, but the three who were appointed in the beginning were not the same three who finalised it, as one by one the original three died, one in fact before he was able to take his oath. They took their oaths – copies of which are at the end of the Inclosure Award – at the White Hart in Retford, or on one occasion at The Bell at Barnby Moor.

The first three Commissioners were John Hutton from Gainsborough, Henson Kirkby from Worksop and Robert Rhodes from Serlby, who would be the first to take the oath. The three who finalised it were William Mason from Eaton, George Kelk from

Carlton, and Thomas Whitaker from Worksop. The first three commissioners took their oaths on 28 June 1776, and the final deed was 'Inrolled in His Majesty's Court of Common Pleas at Westminster dated this 21st day of January 1779'. Thus this huge task took only two and a half years.

It is difficult to understand how the Commissioners organised their task, as it was so complex, onerous and time-consuming. Unfortunately only two Nottinghamshire Minute books were kept by other Commissioners in other areas; these detailed how they worked and actually quoted prices. However, in possessing even two, Nottinghamshire is more fortunate than any of its neighbours; neither the British Museum nor the Public Record Office has any, nor are there any in the collections of the London School of Economics.

So all we have to go on is the Act itself. On reading it one is so impressed with the fine detail – literally every possible situation is covered and no one is left with any uncertainty as to what they are entitled to or what their duties are.
They divided up the land according to Quality, Quantity, Situation and Value', staked out the highways, detailed public bridle roads, footways and drains, etc, in incredible detail.

Landowners of the Time
Many landowners were named and I have outlined a few details about those I was able to research. John Hewett was the first to be mentioned and was one of the petitioners to the Act. He was the Lord of the Manor of Oswaldbeck Soke and is quoted as having 'immemorially enjoyed 120 sheep gates or pasturage for 120 sheep at all times of the year on the said Welham Whinley's Common and that there are divers parcels of inclosed land lying within each of the said townships and that the said John Hewett is the Lord of the

Manor of Oswaldbeck Soke in the said County of Nottingham within, and of which manor the said townships of Clareborough and Welham lie'.

In reference books there is only one manor of such a name and this was in North Wheatley, where it was noted that there is a small stream on the south side of this parish, known as the Oswald Beck, with which the original Oswaldbeck Soke may be connected.

Oswaldbeck Soke comprised the area of country in the North East of Nottingham between the River Idle and the Trent. A Soke has been defined as the right in Anglo-Saxon and early English law to hold court and administer justice with the franchise to receive certain fees or fines arising from it. It was a separate administration and apparently was bounded on the south by the places we now know as East and West Markham. The county of the South Umbrians or Ambrose, a tribe of old Saxons, may have included Oswaldbeck.

The next to be mentioned is Lord Charles Cavendish who was 'im proprietor of the rectory of Clareborough aforesaid and intitled to the great tithes within the said townships'.

Lord Charles Cavendish was born in 1704 and died in 1783. He was a British nobleman, politician and scientist. He was the youngest son of William Cavendish, second Duke of Devonshire and Rachel Russell. In 1727 Lord Charles married Lady Anne Grey, daughter of Henry Grey, first Duke of Kent; they had two children, Henry and Frederick. Henry was considered one of the most accomplished physicists and chemists of his era. Charles Cavendish entered the House of Commons for Heylesbury in 1725 and would remain a member in various seats until 1741 when he turned the family seat of Derbyshire over to his nephew, William Cavendish. In 1757 the Royal Society, of which he was Vice President, awarded him the

Copley medal for his work in the development of thermometers which recorded the maximum and minimum temperatures they had reached.

The Duke of Devonshire is mentioned next as 'patron of the vicarage of Clareborough'.

The Duke of Devonshire's title has been held by members of the Cavendish family, which has been one of the richest and most influential aristocratic families in England, since the sixteenth century. The fifth Duke of Devonshire served as Lord Lt of Derbyshire from 1782 to 1811, but is best remembered for his first marriage to Lady Georgiana Spencer, the celebrated beauty and society hostess who was also an active political campaigner when women's suffrage was still over a century away. She is also famous for her catastrophic affairs and love of gambling. Even though her own family, the Spencers, and her husband's family, the Cavendishes, were immensely wealthy, she was reported to have died deeply in debt because they did not give her any money. She died aged forty-eight, and owed today's equivalent of £3 million. The Duchess was so petrified of her husband discovering the extent of her debts that she kept them a secret. When he discovered the amount, he remarked 'Is that all?'!

Four curates were listed as landowners, all from the parish of Ordsall, which was in the charge of curates as the Rector had other appointments and lived elsewhere.

There was the Rev Joshua Flint 1769 to 1822, who 'is the vicar of the said parish and in right of the said vicarage is intitled to the tithes of osiers, hops and hop poles, and all the sundry tithes arising within the same townships'. He actually lived in Clarborough. Other clerics mentioned were the Rev John Shaw, 'curate of the parish of West Burton', the Rev Richard Norton MA, 'vicar of East

11

Retford,' his patron being the Duke of Devonshire, and also the Rev William Booth, 'vicar of Elkslay, whose patrons were the bailiffs and Burgesses of East Retford, all in the County of Nottingham in right of their said churches'.

Earl Fitzwilliam is mentioned next, as are Samuel Thorold, Robert Mower, Mrs Mary Jerom, Hollis Otter, David Wheelwright, Edward Brown, Richard Hutchinson, John Whitaker, Vincent Fletcher, 'and several others.' It has been difficult to find out much about them all, other than Earl Fitzwilliam (1748 – 1833), was 'styled Viscount Milton until 1756', and was a British Whig statesman of the late eighteenth and early nineteenth centuries. He played a leading part in Whig politics until the 1820s. He led a charmed life: he was educated at Eton and travelled extensively on 'the Grand Tour', which was the expected pursuit of the rich nobleman at this time. He took his seat in the House of Lords and eventually inherited estates which made him one of the greatest landowners in the county, owning Wentworth House, the Malton Estates, an Irish estate and some coal mines.

He was very hardworking and cared deeply for the people. He was a generous landlord, reducing rents and cancelling arrears in bad times as well as supplying cheap food and giving free coal and blankets to the elderly.

He played hard too, enjoying the life of a country gentleman, hunting, horse-breeding, and being a patron of the turf. At the Doncaster races in 1827 the Duke of Devonshire turned up on the first day with a coach-and- six and twelve outriders, the same as Fitzwilliam. Fitzwilliam appeared the next day 'with two coaches and six, and 16 outriders and has kept this thing up ever since'.

As a sign of the lavish times, for some, when the Prince of Wales and the Duke of York toured the North of England in late 1789 they went to the racecourse in Fitzwilliam's carriage, and entering the city of York it was carried by the crowd rather than horses. They were then received by Fitzwilliam at Wentworth House for a lavish party with forty thousand people enjoying a festival in the estate. It was described as '...the true style of ancient English hospitality. His gates were thrown open to the loyalty and love of the surrounding county... The diversions, consisting of all the rural sports in use in that part of the kingdom lasted the whole day and the Prince with the nobility and gentry who were the noble Earl's guests participated in the merriment'. The ball was said to be '... the most brilliant ever seen beyond the Humber'.

I was able to establish that Samuel Thorold lived in Welham and was the son of John Thorold and Elizabeth Hayton. He married Susannah Goodacre, daughter of Samuel Goodacre, on 13 September 1776. He died on 18 January 1825.

In our Clarborough Church, inside the altar rails to the North, there used to be an epitaph (now, sadly, removed) to the third and fourth sons of Samuel Thorald, stating 'Sacred to the memory of John Thorald of Welham Esq. ob June 14, 1812 aged 29 years: of the Rev Charles Thorald late of Peterhouse Cambridge ob May 9, 1820 age 32 years: the third and fourth Sons of Samuel Thorald Esq. and of Susannah his wife. Also to the memory of Mrs Elizabeth Goodacre ob September 13, 1815 aged 95 years, the mother of the above Susannah Thorald'.

Outside the altar rails was a monument to Samuel Thorold himself; this said, 'Sacred to the memory of Samuel Thorold of Welham Esq. son of the late Sir John Thorald bart of Cranwell in the County of Lincoln, died 18th of January 1825 in the 76th year of his age'.

Other oddments I gleaned from the Inclosure Award was that Mrs Mary Jerom – mentioned as one of the landowners at that time –

owned the Well House, which since early times had been a celebrated spring called St John's Well and was a large bath, famous for many cures. A certain John Hutchinson in the early 1700s erected a cottage adjoining the well and enclosed it to preserve it from injury. In olden times a fair or feast was held annually on St John's Day to which the neighbouring villagers came to enjoy sports and games.

Evidently quite recently school outings used to visit the well, described in the 1930s as,
'a flight of steps goes down to the water in a stone basin 12 ft. Square'.
The more popular spas took over in the early nineteenth century.

Mary Outybridge is mentioned in the Act and there was also mention of her in the Clarborough Church under the gallery, at the west end in a mural monument surmounted by a female figure weeping over an urn, with a long inscription underneath.

There is very little left of the mural monument, just a female figure weeping over an urn, and there is no inscription.
(Photo by John Sutton, by kind permission of the Rev. Mark Cantrill)

As a sad reminder of the times, the whole inscription concerning the Outybridge family is included showing how the early death of one's children was to be expected and born nobly. So here was the inscription with Mary's name at the end as the only surviving child of the family:

'Here has interred the body of THOMAS OUTYBRIDGE, late of Bollam House, who died 27 August, 1772 aged 43 years. CATHERINE the daughter of the said Thomas Outybridge and Catherine his wife died 9 July, 1766, aged five months. THOMAS their son died 15 July 1771 aged five months. MILDRED their daughter died 26 December 1772 aged three years and 10 months, Catherine their daughter, died 1 January, 1773 aged seven months. Not lost, but gone before. In a dormitory beneath this place are deposited the earthly remains of Mary Outybridge, the only surviving child of the said Thomas Outybridge and Catherine his wife, she departed this life 21st of August,1808, aged 41 years.'

There was then a sad poem, followed by 'After a weary pilgrimage on earth here rests the remains of Catherine Harrison mother of the above named children, who she humbly hopes to meet in Heaven, died 18 September aged 78'.

Details in the Inclosure Act

After stating the amount of land to be enclosed, 833 acres in Clarebrough and 350 acres in Welham, and naming the landowners, already discussed, the meticulous listing of all the instructions are outlined.

First of all it notes that because all of the land is 'intermixed and dispersed in small parcels' between many people it would be an advantage if the land were 'divided and inclosed' and 'a satisfaction made' to the previous owners for losing the tithes which used to be paid to them. In those days a tithe was considered to be one-tenth part of your produce from land and stock and had to be given to the landowner. This practice now had to cease.

The Commissioners 'considered the Quality, Quantity, Situation and Value of each Proprietors share thereof' and staked out the several public roads or highways, drains, ditches, tunnels and land, and then gave notice of a public meeting on the door of the Parish Church of 'Clarebrough', upon the market crosses of Gainsborough and East Retford and in the *Nottingham Journal*. They then produced a map and schedule of their allotments with a copy for each person to give out at the meeting where they would then hear 'objections complaints and disputes'. Incredibly there were none and so it was finally put in writing upon '30 skins of Parchment'.

We have viewed the original skins of parchment now housed in the Archives in Nottingham. They are now difficult to read, but wonderfully preserved, rolled and wrapped in a linen cloth.

One can hardly believe with such a complex task that there was no dissent, particularly, as stated; initially not everyone was in favour of enclosure.

This shows the original skins of parchment of the Enclosure Act.
By kind permission of the Nottinghamshire Archives. Ref EA42/
(Photo by John Sutton)

Of interest to us are the mention of names used today, namely Gainsborough Road, Welham Road and Sturton Road. Howbeck Lane and Gill Green Close were also mentioned. No detail was left to chance. Public bridle roads were listed and it even described how footways were to be used – for foot only with stiles and gates maintained properly and planks with a rail to be erected over ditches. Previous private roads were now to be used by everyone.

It is fascinating to read the detail describing the route that each road should follow. Public bridleways were detailed as having to be '30 feet between the ditches' and for some reason others had to be 33 feet – such was the exactitude!

Public drains had to be made and each had to be of a certain measurement. One had to be 'Nine feet wide at the top, 4 feet wide at the bottom and 3 feet all deep below the surface'. Others had different dimensions but most precisely described. They had to be cleaned, maintained and kept up by the constable of Clareborough.

It has to be noted here that until the early nineteenth century the churchwardens appointed parish constables to impose law and order. Constables were private citizens elected every year at the parish vestry meeting. If there were incidents that the parish constable could not cope with they could call on any able-bodied person to help. They had a whistle and everyone was expected to chase the person until they caught him (hence the phrase 'hue and cry'). It was an offence not to help. It was not a popular post as it was unpaid and often served in turn.

Fence ditches were to be called private drains and had to be cut open, scoured and cleansed by the owners so that the water could flow freely into the public drains. Public drains had to be scoured, cleansed and deepened between 21 September and 21 October by the constable. There was a penalty of five shillings for every seven yards of public drains and two shillings for every seven yards of private drains neglected.

Tunnels had to be made where water was required to go across roads and maintained by the Surveyors of the Highways or by the proprietors. If the tunnel or wathstead was neglected, twenty shillings was charged to the Surveyors by the magistrate or ten shillings to private owners. The charging of maintaining public drains or sewers, tunnels or wathsteads had to be contributed to by the owners or occupiers, and if one refused, after fourteen days the sum was doubled and all monies collected were used by the Surveyors for repairs.

The Church was very much the hub of the village, as all the Surveyors, yearly on Easter Monday in the Public Vestry, had to account for the rents and let out the herbage or pasture for the best rent possible. To help preserve the fences which had been erected none of the roads or ways were to be let for pasture for any horses, sheep lambs or other cattle for ten years.

Having allotted and decided upon the public, and private roads, public drains and sewers, it then details the allotment of land to each person, being most specific about the area in question. It also depended on the tithes which the owners used to receive, and the value of their previously owned land. The new owners with their enclosed property were now informed of the rent they had to pay in compensation for the tithes they used to pay.

For example a certain George Brown was the part-owner of Hop Yard Close and now was discharged of any tithes he used to pay to Lord Charles Cavendish and now had to pay seven shillings annually as compensation, i.e. as rent. It was paid by four equal quarterly payments. Part of the Hop Yard Close was also previously owned by the vicar and so George also had to pay 1s. 6d. to the vicar.

It might be an opportune moment here to discuss the Hops Industry. In Nottinghamshire the hop-growing area stretched from Retford to Southwell and was known as the 'North Clays' district on account of its position north of the Trent and of the heavy nature of the loams developed from the Keuper Marl. This is an obsolete name for multiple layers of mudstone and siltstone of the Triassic age, which proved good for hop-growing. Some thirty-five parishes contained hop yards.

The area to the west of Retford and Tuxford, known as 'The Dukeries', contained the homes of several titled persons, and their connections with the south of England may have induced initial experiments. When the hops were grown on a small, even domestic scale in Nottinghamshire it was, 'in vallies and wet lands for the most part, not very valuable for other purposes'. Retford, as the most northerly hop fair in the country, was of special importance until the breaking down of traditional economic ways with the advent of rail transport.

At one point in the eighteenth century it is recorded that landlords in Nottinghamshire ordered their tenants to reduce their hop acreage, 'fancying that hop grounds were enriching the growers............without benefiting themselves in any way'. Hop-growing was not so lucrative as is generally supposed, for production costs were six or seven times that for a comparable area of grain, and a heavy excise duty had to be paid, quite apart from the risk involved in growing a delicate plant that was vulnerable to pests and diseases.

A certain William Batten also owned part of Hop Yard Close and also had to pay 1s. 6d. to the vicar. It also states that Vincent Fletcher owned Broad Gores Close and two 'small parcels', called the Hop Yards. He had to pay Lord Charles Cavendish the annual composition rent of 11s. 10d. in four quarterly payments.

The vicar accepted altogether the payment of £2 19s. 10d. from thirteen annual rents in lieu of previous tithes. However, throughout the Act it is stressed that the vicar is the only person who still collects tithes: 'However the tithes of all such Oziers Hops and Hop Poles as may herafter grow or arise theron which are to remain payable in KIND as before the passing of the said Act and Mortuaries Surplice Fees and Easter Offerings only excepted.'

The Act also shared out the remaining open arable fields and meadows, common stinted pasture and other waste ground. It was to be staked out by the Surveyors and they could use it from 14 October when the Act was passed. Before 1 April it had to be well ditched and fenced. Each fence was precisely named as quoted here: 'and we do order and direct that ____ and his heirs shall make out and at all times hereafter maintain and keep in repair the ____ fence of the said allotment'.

It had to be planted with ' Good Quickwood', three and a half feet from the stakes and fences at one side with 'good post and double rails'. Various agricultural articles in history books call the quickwood fence an 'enclosure hedge', and state that it was the best form of hedging 'as they plant the quickwood in 3 strata of earth and give it the advantage of deriving its nourishment from a deep soil which always catches every shower'. The ditches had to be three feet at least and they were fined 5s. for every acre neglected.

The Act is so detailed that it can certainly be referred to in times of doubt, and has been over the years. This was noted in a question referred to in the Parish Councils Minute Book, dated April 1899, when a disgruntled constable asked if it really was his duty to clean all parish dykes. He was informed that indeed, according to the Act, that was what he had to do.

Near the end of the Act it categorically states that on 14 October 1777 the proprietors have accepted their said allotments 'in full bar of and satisfaction of and for the several pieces and parcels of Ground which immediately before such Division and Allotment belonged to such proprietors respectively and were then dispersed in the said Open Fields Meadows or Stinted Pastures and in full bar of and in satisfaction for their several and respective Pasture Gates, Common Rights, and other Rights and Property is over ....'.

Chapter Two

The Old Parish Council Minute Books

The oldest Minute Book in the Clarborough and Welham Parish Office dates back to December 1894 and was used until April 1940. It is now a little battered and faded, but still a wonderful record of some of the occasions, problems and decisions in which the Parish Council were involved. There are also two others relating to events up to 2008. As the greatest interest is in the happenings in the past I decided that I would comment only up to 1950.

(Photo by
John Sutton)

On occasions it has been difficult to read the writing and so I apologise in advance for any mistakes in my interpretation! In the interests of those who have long-standing families in the village I have listed the members of the very first meeting to be referred to in the old leather book.

1894

The first Parish Council Meeting was held in the School Room, Clarborough on December 31 1894. At this meeting sixteen names were put forward and seconded to be voted on to become Parish Councillors and the votes duly recorded in the leather book. The final Councillors were as follows:

Martin Buck – Clarborough – Chairman

Charles Edward de More Thorald – Welham – Vice Chairman and Treasurer

Mr Spencer as Assistant Overseer – Clerk

Joseph Bartle – Clarborough

John Marriott – Clarborough

Walter Saul – Bolham Cottage

John Stephenson – Tiln

John Wistow – Clarborough

At the end of that first meeting Mr Spencer was 'empowered to obtain all the necessary books', and it was agreed that the Chairman should call a meeting 'when necessary'.

1895

The next meeting was in March 1895, at which, from our modern point of view, they made the surprising decision that all the meetings of the Council should be in private. They then elected three constables for Clarborough and Welham, one being a Councillor and two others from the villages.

Note: until the early nineteenth century the churchwardens appointed parish constables to impose law and order. Constables were private citizens elected every year at the parish vestry meeting. If there were incidents that the parish constable could not cope with they would call on any able-bodied person to help.

At the same meeting it is interesting to note that a certain George Stephenson was to be paid 1s. 6d for his services in preparing for the meeting. He had to prepare the room, fire, and lights when necessary, and to leave the room 'in such order as not to interfere with the teaching of the school'.

Allotments were requested, so a letter was written to the vicar asking if he and his tenant were willing to let the field belonging to the vicar so that the Council could provide allotments. However, the vicar stated that he could not meet their wishes, so no land could be offered for allotments. This matter kept recurring and one Councillor at the next meeting offered some of his land subject to the approval of his landlord. A public meeting was called for anyone interested in allotments as seven people had already intimated their interest. However, at the meeting in January 1896 only three applicants attended and no further steps were taken. At that same meeting all the charities of the parish were to be thoroughly investigated.

1896
There are many incidents in the Minute Book referring to drains, dykes, etc needing cleaning, and in January there was a drainage problem down the Smeath.

There is also the entertaining description of there being 'the dangerous position of persons driving through the bridge at night-time'. The railway company, the Great Central, was asked to fit a red light in order that persons driving through the bridge at night might be warned of the approach of trains from the direction of the tunnel. This is also referred to in February 1898 when they request the company to have a flag in the daytime and a signal of some kind on the bridge after sunset. In March the company wrote that they 'could not accede to the request of the Council to place a signal on Welham Bridge', so, as this was felt to be unsatisfactory, other councils were to be asked to join in.

Note: the railway line was built for the Manchester, Sheffield and Lincolnshire Railway (MS and LR), opening in 1849. MS and LR changed its name to Great Central Railway (GCR) in 1897 and in 1923 the GCR was grouped in the London and North Eastern Railway. The bridge MAC3/203 (a modern rail track designation) dates essentially from the 1840s. When the railway network was developing in the mid-nineteenth century, road transport was extremely rudimentary compared to today. Sometimes people went to the Welham sidings to collect parcels.

There are references every year to 'Lane letting' and in April of this year it was proposed that the money be used for the repairs of the byways and the large drain running through the village. The letting initially was always on Easter Monday and the local auctioneer was used. Later it was changed to Easter Tuesday.

1897

Two Parish Councillors were to attend Hayton's Parish Council to discuss their clearing out Smeath Lane drains and clearing the Smeath of bushes. In March the Parish Councillors asked the District Council's permission to use their steamroller to improve Clarborough Parish roads.

In April they brought forward the question of celebrating the Diamond Jubilee and a public meeting was to be held. Sadly we do not hear what the celebrations involved!

1898

A newly elected Assistant Overseer was to give a bond of £100 as security for the proper performance of his duties.

In April of this year there is the delightful comment when the constables were chosen that 'the handcuffs and staff were handed over to Mr Joseph Bartle'. There is reference to this on page 18.

At that meeting they also decided that smoking was to be permitted for those who wished to do so.

1899

In March this year there were various road problems – Bluestocking Lane and Cherry Holt Road – and also the hedges and ditches thereabouts.

There were also complaints about the Clarborough cesspool. In April there appeared to be a disgruntled constable who asked the Parish Award (Enclosure Act) to be searched to see whether it was the duty of the constables to clean all parish dykes. In December the Clerk read a 'lengthy report' taken from the Parish Award (Enclosure Act) respecting the public and private drains of the parish. After considerable discussion it was proposed and carried that the Constable did indeed attend to the Dykes 'as heretofore'.

There was a proposal that land should be purchased for a siding at Welham with a copy of the petition to Parliament for this compulsory power to purchase. The Council stated that they would give the railway company every possible assistance. Sadly, in 1901 the company replied and regretted that they could not give any facilities for a station to be erected. In 1905 there was still agitation supporting this.

1900

In June there were comments concerning the Bone Mill Bridge: the Canal Company had always repaired the frontage to this bridge and the Parish, for over fifty years, had repaired the lane.

1901

In 1901 a resolution was passed concerning the death of Queen Victoria. It read: 'The members of this Parish Council desire to record their deep sense of the great loss to the nation by the death of our beloved Queen Victoria, and they heartily congratulate King Edward VII on his accession to the throne, and trust that he might have a glorious reign and follow in the steps of his illustrious mother'.

There was also a comment calling the attention of the Parish Councillors to the fact that sods had been cut off the herbage belonging to the parish by the Retford Race Committee; so they wrote to the Secretary of the Race Committee reminding him that permission should be sought. Evidently Spencers and Sons had asked the Council to sell the Clarborough proportion of the Smeath, but they were advised that the council had no powers to sell.
Money matters are always of interest and when the Lane letting was resolved in March it was commented that the auctioneer was to be paid 10s. 6d, 'the usual terms', for his efforts.

In April there was a deputation from Hayton regarding the question of payment of a share of the vicar's tithe upon the Smeath.

1902

There is frequent mention of the Parish Award, which the archivists at the Nottinghamshire Archives assure me is the same as the Enclosure Act, and in January a complaint is received about the ploughing-up of the public footpath in the Church field and the road's being obstructed. The offender had his attention drawn to the illegality of such a proceeding and was quoted the section of the Act of Parliament respecting the same.

New J.Ps were to be appointed and it was suggested that Mr Thorald's name be put forward to the Lord-Lieutenant, who, at this time, was the Duke of Portland. Sir Frederick Milner was to be asked to support the application.

In March they decided to consider the question of the Coronation Festivities at the next meeting and in April they called a public meeting for May to discuss celebrating the Coronation of Edward VII.

1903

In June the Clerk reported that he had received a circular from NCC relating to the appointment of School Managers for the Clarborough Day School; this would supersede the present School Board. The Council was asked to nominate two persons and recommend the names of four others to be elected. This was duly done.

1904

At the March meeting the usual Lane letting was resolved, but this time to be held at The Black Woman Inn.

Note: The Black Woman was the first public house to disappear from the village. It was located opposite the Kings Arms and was part of what was known as Old Oak Cottage, on the left-hand side of the driveway that now leads to the village hall. It was reportedly one of the oldest buildings in the village. The last publican was a Mr Otter. After use as a public house it became a bakery, general store and fish-and-chip shop. The building stood right next to the main road but was demolished in the early 1920s, providing a small garden for the remaining dwelling house.

1905

In January the Clerk and Assistant Overseer was asked to make a new valuation list for the parish as the previous one had not been accepted by the Assessment Committee. Some hours were spent on this and in March the Clerk asked for extra remuneration for his work and was allowed £5 above his normal wage.

1906
In December it was reported that the bond given by the Treasurer was insufficient, as the Act of Parliament required a bond equivalent to a certain rate. After some discussion £87 was decided upon.

1907
In April concern was expressed over the state of Gringley Balk Road, which the District had taken over, repaired, but lately done nothing about. It was stated that 'The road is much used by the general public, by the schoolchildren of Little Gringley who attend Clarborough Sunday and Day schools and by the Little Gringley people who attend Clarborough Church'.The Council evidently considered it an 'unawarded road', but the award map was referred to as being difficult to understand and so the Parish Council was in a bit of a quandary.

1908
In March the Parish Councillors were asked to nominate a candidate for the office of Rural District Councillor; they did so and Mr Bartle was agreed upon. An important notice was reported at this meeting from the Nottinghamshire Quarter Sessions – held in Nottingham – that stated that it had been decided to abolish the annual election of parish constables on the grounds that they were now obsolete.

Note: the County and Borough Police Act in 1856 made policing compulsory throughout England and Wales and made provision for Treasury assistance to local authorities. By 1900 the number of police in England, Wales and Scotland totalled 46,800 working in 243 separate forces.

1910
There was an entertaining extra written in the October minutes, which were sent to the Rural District Council, to the effect that 'The

Parish Council of Clarborough acting for, and on behalf of the ratepayers, strongly protest against the expenditure of a large sum of money being voted for the purchase of a motor car for the use of the Rural District Council's Surveyor, as extravagant and an unnecessary expense. They are also of the opinion that as the Surveyor receives a very handsome salary for the services he renders, if a motorcycle or car is deemed necessary by him to carry out his duties then he should purchase the machine himself'.
So there!

1911

As has been noted before, there are a few instances of the Parish Councillors deciding upon festivities for various royal occasions. Here it is for the Coronation of King George V. Again, sadly, we never hear a description of the celebrations.

At the end of March there is posted therein a newspaper cutting from the Clarborough Parish Council: they 'strongly and unanimously protest against the proposed rating area for the new Secondary School at Retford, at a cost of over £10,000, for the following reasons:

- There is no necessity for the proposed school.
- That the increasing demands from the Nottinghamshire County Council for education and other expenses are becoming an extremely heavy burden on the ratepayers.
- That the amount proposed to be spent on the new school is most extravagant, and that the proposed rateable area is anything but a fair and equitable one. There are many parishes left out of the area that might benefit by the new school.
- This Parish Council does not consider that Clarborough will benefit in the smallest degree by the erection of this proposed school'.

1912

In April a complaint was received from a gentleman who had purchased one of the parish lanes for growing crops and had discovered a neighbour, 'eating the herbage' from his land. The Clerk was told to write to the miscreant and threaten legal proceedings!

1913

In March the managers of the school were asked to appoint another teacher, but decided that, 'owing to the extraordinarily small numbers of children on the schoolbooks viz 45', they did not fill the vacancy which had just arisen, and that they considered the head teacher and her sister were sufficient for the school's needs.

1914

In March there was a deputation from the Hayton Parish Councillors regarding the two portions of the Smeath belonging to Clarborough and Hayton: Hayton had five-eighths of the land, compared to three-eighths belonging to Clarborough and therefore they should have their share of the rent according to the acreage. They threatened to erect a fence if their request was not agreed to. Clarborough Parish Councillors asked for twelve months notice of the change in the mode of letting.

Between the years of 1914 and 1918 there was a very quiet period for obvious reasons.

1918

In March there was discussion about the damage and annoyance caused by sparrows and it was decided to try to suppress the nuisance by offering 1/2d. per head for sparrows and 1d. for a nest of four eggs. The Byways Surveyor was to collect and pay for the same. Mrs Freda Robinson of Welham remembers her grandmother making sparrow pie for which about fifty sparrows were needed!

A circular was read out asking the Councillors to encourage allotments among the workingmen of the parish, but as there were no allotments in the parish and most of the labourers had good gardens it was deemed that no action needed to be taken. (A later circular was read out in 1931 stating the same but still there were no applications for allotments).

There was a complaint about a heap of manure and stones obstructing Whitsun Pie Lock Lane and the miscreant was firmly advised to remove it or face further action!

In May the vicar asked for the consent of the Parish Councillors to divide a footpath in order to extend the churchyard.

1920

In March it was decided that at the Lane letting the herbage only be let and eaten up to 31 October in each year.

Upon reading a circular regarding allowing fire engines to attend fires the following resolution was passed: 'That in the opinion of this meeting it is highly desirable that immediate arrangements should be made by the Retford Rural District Council respecting fires that may break out in the Council's area and they trust that each parish will at once strengthen the hands of the Council by passing similar resolutions'.

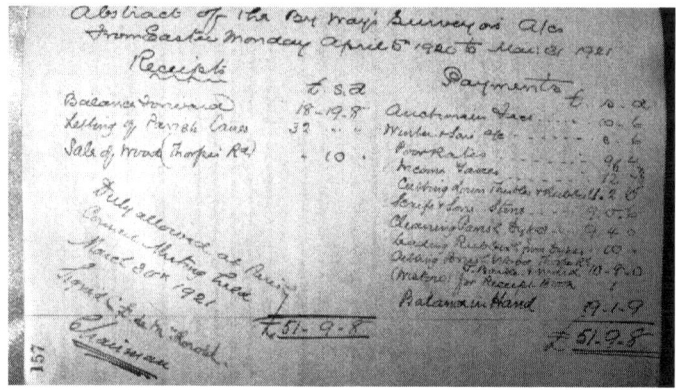

The surveyor's accounts for 1921,
(by kind permission of Clarborough and Welham Parish Council)

1921

A pleasant little comment was made in April regarding the vicar's yew tree: 'The Clerk was instructed to call the vicar of Clarborough's attention, in a friendly way, to the yew hedge at the vicarage which has grown across the dyke which is dangerous to cattle passing up and down the lanes owing to the poisonous nature'.

1924

In May there was a letter from the postmaster of Retford asking for the opinion of the Council respecting a half-holiday to be given weekly to the postman who brought the letters from Retford. This was agreed.

A circular was read from the County respecting the safe custody of the Parish Award (Enclosure Act): it should be deposited in Nottingham. However, the Council decided to arrange for it to be looked after at the Westminster Bank.

1925

In April it was asked that the Retford Rural District Council's attention be drawn to the danger to schoolchildren at the corner of Church Road (Lane?) adjoining the wheelwright's shop, and to the state of the dyke protection (several of the rods and posts in the dyke were broken). In 1930 a similar decision was made to send a note to Notts County Council regarding the protection from serious incident to schoolchildren at Church Road (Lane?) corner as there had been many narrow escapes.

At a special meeting in November the Government Bill relating to their proposal to take the 'valuation and rating question' into their hands instead of the Assessment Committees performing the duties was discussed. They strongly opposed the Bill in its present form as 'it would not be any advantage either to the Poor Law or Rating Authorities.'

1927

'As overseers were now extinct in regards to the duties of assessing the various properties of the parish the meeting elected two persons according to the New Act, which came into operation on April 1, to assist the Rating and Assessment Committee authorities of the Retford Union if called upon to do so.'

This now reflected upon the Clerk's salary in lieu of his office as Assistant Overseer and it was later decided to pay him £2 10s. per year.

Money-wise, it was interesting to note that the Clerk was reimbursed by £1 for having to travel to Nottingham to attend the Rating and Assessment Authority's meeting.

1928

In May the Chairman introduced the question of supplying the Parish Council area with electricity from Retford, 'which he strongly advocated'. It was agreed upon and they requested to find out the cost of five electric lamps which could be obtained.

1930

In April there was a reply from the Rural District Council concerning a query about removing bricks from the Welham Pinfold, the answer being that no person has the right to remove bricks forming the Pinfold.

In June the Council were informed that the Notts Boundary Committee would meet in relation to extending the Borough of Retford to include Clarborough and other places in the immediate locality. This did not please the councillors and so the following resolution was passed: 'At a meeting of the Clarborough Parish Council held on June 6, 1930 the suggestion of the East Retford Corporation to extend the Borough Boundary to include Clarborough and Other Rural Parishes was thoroughly discussed. It was resolved that the Parish Council of Clarborough strongly object to any change of boundaries being made until the effect of the proposed changes was fully explained by the Corporation and the County Council and even then the matter should be subject to a referendum of the whole of the voters of the Parish'. A sad little reflection was noted concerning the sum of £5 16s., which had been realised by letting the lanes: this sum would only just cover the expenses for clearing out the worst places in the parish drains.

1931
Notts County Council's attention was drawn to the dangerous state of the road leading to the school. A public meeting was held in December to consider the question of lighting by electricity the main road from Welham Corner to Clarborough post office. At the meeting the cost per lamp and the probable amount of additional rates required was discussed. It was decided by twenty-six votes to three not to adopt the scheme.

1934
In March the Council wrote to the Retford Rural District asking for figures of estimated cost for providing water for the parish from the schemes outlined for Wheatley, Hayton and Retford.

1935
In March it was decided that to celebrate the King's Silver Jubilee a tea and sports day should be given to the children of Clarborough and Welham and that a committee be formed to carry out the same. They decided to invite Hayton to join in the forthcoming celebrations.

1936
In February the Clerk was instructed to write to the postmaster, drawing his attention to the great need for a public telephone kiosk for Clarborough and District. In December it was proposed that four lamps be situated: one at Welham Corner, one at Church Lane,

one near the shops in the village street and one at the bottom of Clarborough Hill.

Notts County Council was asked to establish a 30 mph speed limit through the village from Church Road to the bottom of Clarborough Hill.

Notts County Council were asked to make the Clarborough Institute a polling station in lieu of the school, as the Institute was close to the highway and much better lit.

The Clerk was instructed to write to the Postal Authority urging them to have the 'already promised' telephone kiosk erected as early as possible.

1937

A special meeting was held in the Clarborough Institute in January to consider the following proposals:

'To adopt the Street Lighting Act of 1833.

To consider the provision of at least four electric lamps at dangerous points in the main street.... at a cost of three pounds each lamp per year, that is one penny increase in the parish rate each half-year'. This was carried. The celebration for King George V1 was to be 'carried out on similar lines as on the last occasion'.

1938

In October it was proposed that three additional lamps be erected: another one at Welham, one at Bone Mill Lane and one two thirds down Big Lane. This was agreed at a parish meeting later that month. There was also an Air Raid Precaution circular noted regarding the evacuation of the civil population and the Council decided that the Institute be the reception room for such a situation, and a reception officer was appointed; a billeting officer was also appointed.

A circular was handed round in connection with the Adult Education Department of University College, Nottingham, regarding a series of talks on topics in general; a meeting was to be held in the Institute later that month.

1939

Notts County Council asked for the Parish Award (Enclosure Act) to be sent to the Shire Hall for safekeeping; this was agreed.

1940

One of the last comments in the old leather Minute Book was regarding the collection of waste paper. To help in this situation the schoolmistress was to be informed, as well as the chief scoutmaster. A central depot for collection was decided upon. This was the last comment of note in the old Minute Book, and at one time this was when the study was to be finished. However, in the next Minute Book there are interesting comments concerning the situation during the war, and so I have extended the study to 1950.

1942

At the February meeting a letter was read out concerning Warship Week to which the Council determined to give all possible aid.

1943

In April a letter regarding the Wings for Victory Campaign was read out and it was decided to call a parish meeting, together with the Savings Group Collectors, to organise 'a strong Committee of those willing workers' to help make it a success.

In November it was noted that the Wings for Victory Campaign had been an outstanding success and that £6020 had been invested in war loans and £720 9s. 7d. had been loaned to the Government interest-free, 'such money to be used for assisting men from the forces'.

The Rural District Council awarded a replica of a plaque and this was hung in the Institute.

1944

In April it was reported that a 'Salute the Soldier' campaign was to be held in the Retford and Rural Area from 3 to 10 June 1944 and the target hoped for was £300,000. A public meeting was to be called to discuss the ways and means of achieving this.

1945

In May there was a comment concerning the Lanes letting: prices realised were considered satisfactory especially in view of the shortage of labour for tending the cattle.

In October it was decided that the Council should become a member of the Notts Rural Community Council, the subscription being 10s. per annum.

At the same meeting it was reported that the condition of the parish drains and overhanging hedges needed attention and there was difficulty in obtaining local labour. However, there had been a conversation with the War Agricultural Committee regarding the employment of prisoners of war for this purpose, and in the near future some labour would be available.

1946

In April it was agreed that German prisoners should clean the dyke at a cost of 37s. 6d per chain (66 feet).

In May a discussion was held on how to organise the Victory Celebrations. It was suggested that funds should be collected, and sports, a fancy-dress parade, a whist drive, dance and a tea be held for the children.

A further meeting was called later in the month and it was reported that no funds appeared to be forthcoming. There was money in the Wings for Victory Fund but the trustees of this fund did not agree to the money being used in this way.

In October it was thought that the Council were 'not having a fair deal' as the light at the bottom of Clarborough Hill had not been lit since the end of the war and this had to be put right.

1947

In April a Flood Relief Fund was discussed and it was suggested that a fancy dress dance should be held. At a previous dance a pig was raffled; this raised a lot of money and was to be repeated.

In October there was a comment that no new houses had been built in Clarborough, so this was to be followed up.

In November it was decided that the Council should ask the Rural District Council for six more houses.

It was agreed at the same meeting that some kind of function be held to celebrate Princess Elizabeth's wedding. It was proposed that tea be given for the children followed by a social and dance – again, a pig was given as a raffle.

1948

In January it was noted that Town and Country Planning could not agree to the request for houses as no land was available in the parish. Most interesting to note, for our modern reader, is that a discussion took place regarding a proposed bypass, 'which will cut out all Welham'.

At the same meeting complaints had been made about parcels which came from the Dominions for the old and infirm of the parish and that many had not had any. As these gifts went to the Rural District Council's office it was thought that the Parish Council ought to help in the distribution of these parcels.

It was again reported that no danger sign had as yet been erected at Welham Corner although the matter had been agreed.

In March it was reported that an architect had inspected some sites in the village regarding possible new houses, 'but owing to the proposed bypass and other projects', it was decided that more discussion needed to take place.

1949

The question of houses was being pursued and in the hands of Town and Country Planning. The houses would be let on a points' value and agricultural workers would be first priority.

1950

There was an application for premises to be used as a joiner's shop; this was granted.

The question of a 30 mph speed limit was raised but the police had informed them that nothing could be done until the streetlights were spaced closer together.

Further Minutes are available to read on request at the Parish Office.

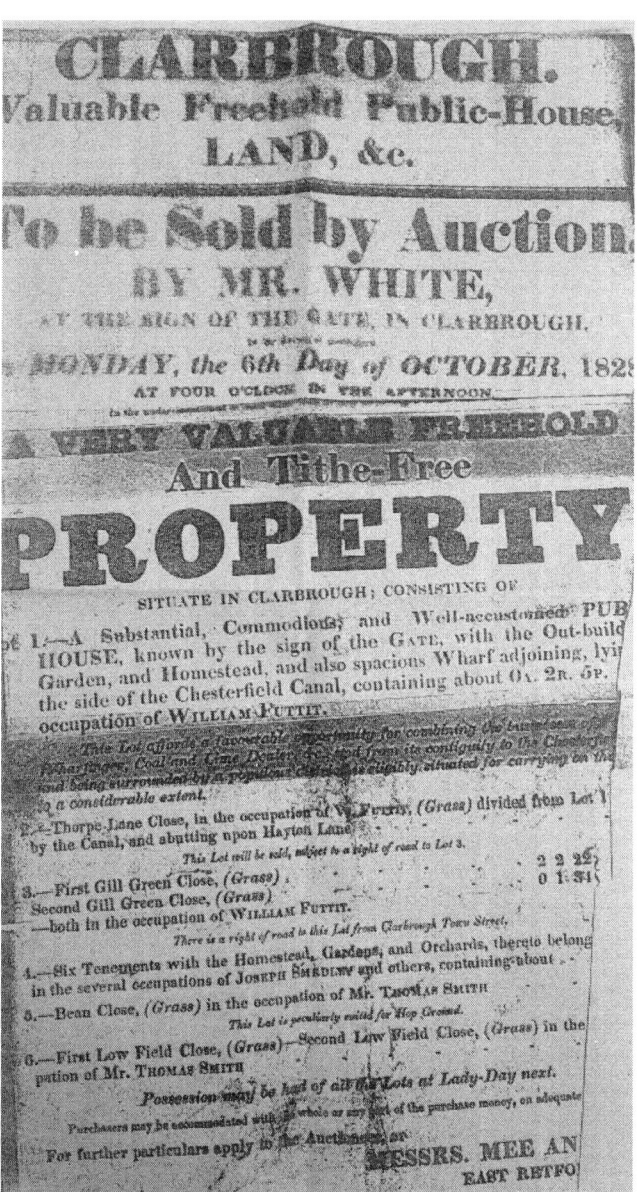

A poster for the auction of The Gate in 1828

41

Chapter Three

A Miscellany from 1828 - 1931

Of interest is a copy of a poster of the auction of The Gate in 1828 (see overleaf). Reproduced here by kind permission of Bassetlaw Museum.

Over the page are details, held in the Bassetlaw Museum, of a Roman bust which was found about 1849. As you can see, it was a marble bust, fourteen inches high; it had been found by a farm labourer. It was in the possession of the late Canon Brookes until his death, when it was purchased by a Mr Henry Hill of Nottingham. It was shown in 1899 at an exhibition of antiquities at the Thoroton Society, but sadly research has found that they have no notification of it in a catalogue and no photograph.

Type of site or object	BUST	Parish (Civil): CLARBOROUGH	County: NOTTS.	No.:

Description (including date or period, with sketch on back)	Exact situation: *Find-spot unknown.*
Clarborough bust, c. 14" high, recorded in VCH Notts as being found by farm labourer c. 1849 & in possession of late Canon Brookes until his death, when purchased by a Mr. Henry Hill of Nottingham. Shown in 1899 at exhibition of antiquities at the Thoroton Society, but present whereabouts unknown.	Map references:
	O.S. 1" · O.S. 6" · Grid (6 figure)
	Type of ground:
	Date when found:
Ref. Retford Times. 14th April 1967. front page. Article by Mr. C. H. Bear.	Name and address of finder and/or informant:
	Present location:

References to publications:	Location of measured drawings, etc.:

Please return one copy of card to :

Type of site or object	ROMAN PORTRAIT BUST	Parish (Civil): CLARBOROUGH	County: Notts	No.:

Description (including date or period, with sketch on back)	Exact situation:
Marble bust, in possession at one time of Canon Brookes of Nottingham when he lived at Clarborough, bought by Mr H. Hill & exhibited 1899 to Thoroton Soc. 14" high probably (3rd. Close cut hair & features suggest it may be Balbinus (A.D. 238)	Map references:
	O.S. 1" · O.S. 6" · Grid (6 figure)
	Type of ground:
	Date when found: circa 1850.
	Name and address of finder and/or informant:
	Present location:

References to publications:	Location of measured drawings, etc.:
TTS 3 p51 No 354.	

The newspaper article (overleaf) from the *Gainsborough and Retford Times*, 14 April 1967, mentions the Roman Bust, bemoaning the fact that the exact site where it was found was never noted – so in fact there could be more exciting finds somewhere in our area – and also the sadness of its 'present whereabouts' being unknown.

Archaeology in North Nottinghamshire

By MR. C. H. BEAR

WITH the proposal to re-establish the Retford Historical and Archaeological Society, the time may well be opportune to place on record the present state of archaelogy and archaeological activity in the Retford area.

For a number of years, North Nottinghamshire has been an archaelogical "dead spot" in so far that very little of any consequence has been undertaken in the area. This has not been due to lack of suitable evidence, but because no co-ordinating body with sufficient support has been in existence.

It is also to be regretted that much of what has come to light in past years has either been lost or gone out of town to museums or into the hands of private individuals and no reports made to the proper authorities.

A classic example of this loss is the famous missing Clarborough Bust. This was of Roman origin, about 14 ins. high and of fine workmanship. It is recorded in the Nottinghamshire Victoria County History as being found by a farm labourer about 1849 and was in the possession of the late Canon Brookes until his death when it was purchased by a Mr. Henry Hill, of Nottingham. It was shown in 1899 at an exhibition of antiquities at the Thoroton Society, but its present whereabouts are unknown.

While we may deplore the fact that this object seems to have been lost, it is equally regrettable that the actual find spot was never recorded as this may well mark an area of considerable achaeological interest.

During the past two or three years there has been an increased activity in field work and excavation in the Retford area. Valuable field surveys by a number of people have revealed many new achaeological sites from pre-historic times through to the mediaeval period. But much more is still to be done, and done quickly if we are not to lose valuable material through building, gravel working and other activities. Archaeological material has certainly been destroyed on the site of the new Cottam Power Station.

One recent find of very great importance has been made by Mr. R. Minnitt, of Laneham, who, on a routine field survey has found a large collection of flint implements, which include a number of finely worked scrapers and leaf shaped arrow heads. This must constitute one of the most important finds of this type ever to be made in North Nottinghamshire.

The valuable excavation work carried out at Rampton last summer by Mr. M. Ponsford, also revealed information of great importance in respect of life in the Trent Valley from about the first century A.D. to well into the Roman Period. This particular site could produce much more evidence by further work.

With this welcome growth of archaeological interest it is perhaps worth mentioning that the present study of the subject extends from prehistoric times right through to the present and no doubt useful work could be done in the Retford area in the field of Industrial Archaeology.

The work of a new society, however, could cover more than archaeology. It could associate itself with many aspects of local history. The possibility of a new society in Retford to deal with these matters is welcome news and it is hoped that everyone who may be interested will make a special effort to attend the public meeting to be held at Eaton Hall on Wednesday, April 19th, at 7.30 p.m.

Notable Residents of Clarborough
and Welham listed between 1848 and 1879

Villagers whose families have lived locally for many years might find it interesting to peruse the names mentioned in the next few pages. Both Kelly's Directory of 1848, and White's Directory of 1853 list the inhabitants of Clarborough and Welham – with some discrepancies, it would appear!

It is fascinating to note their occupations. Wright's Directory of 1879 allows one to study any differences, additions, or removals.

As noted in Wright's Directory in 1879, the 'old' Clarborough included Clarborough, plus the hamlets of Bolham, Welham, Little Gringley Moorgate and Spital Hill.

Clareborough
Smart Rev. George, B.A. [curate]
TRADERS.
Barlow Thomas, *King's Arms inn*
Batty John, farmer
Bell John, farmer
Bingham Robert, farmer
Buck Francis, cattle dealer
Buck Thomas, cattle dealer
Clark Thomas, boot & shoe maker
Downs John, maltster
Freeman John, schoolmaster
Golland Richard, butcher
Hempstock William, blacksmith
Hurt Richard, tailor
Newboult William, shoemaker
Neet John, farmer
Pentfield Thomas, plaster dealer
Pettinger George, *Gate inn*
Rawlinson George, farmer
Rawlinson John, farmer

Rogers Thomas, farmer
Rogers Vincent, shopkeeper
Rogers William, shopkeeper
Smedley Joseph, patten & clog maker
Stephenson Jas. wheelwright, & *Black Girl inn*
Storrs Thomas, cattle dealer
Skelton Joseph, farmer
Young George, *Robin Hood inn*
Walker Robert, miller
Wells John, farmer
Wheat Samuel, boot & shoe maker

Welham.
GENTRY.
Hutchinson Henry Clark, esq
Hutchinson Mrs. Ann
Thorold Charles, esq. Welham villa
TRADERS.
Booth Thomas, farmer
Heeds Robert, *Hop Pole inn*
Hurst George, beer retailer, Winleys

Marsh Edward, beer retailer, Winleys
Wheelwright Thomas, farmer

An entry from Kelly's Directory 1848

CLARBOROUGH.

Bartle Mr. William
Bower John, relieving officer
Clark Thomas, shoemaker
Freeman John, schoolmaster
Hempstock William, blacksmith
Hill James, vict., Black Woman
Hodge Rev. Charles, M. A., vicar,
    Moorgate
Littlewood Geo., collector of taxes
Peatfield Thomas, plaster manufctr
Pettinger George, vict., Gate
Rogers Vincent, shopkeeper
Smedley Joseph, nail maker & vict.,
    Robin Hood
Taylor Joseph, vict., King's Arms
Wait Rbt. & Son, brick & tile mkrs
Walker Richard, corn miller
Wheat Samuel, shoe makers

Farmers.

Batty John
Bell John
Bingham Robert
Bingley G., *Grange*
Buck George, and
    cattle dealer
Buck Thomas, &
    cattle dealer
Champion Joseph
Creighton James
Dunk Charles
Hardy Samuel
Littlewoood Jph
Rogers Thomas
Rollinson George
Skelton Joseph
Taylor William,
    Winleys
Stevenson James,
    (& wheelwright)

White's Directory 1853
(With kind permission of Bassetlaw Museum)

CLAREBOROUGH is an extensive parish, adjoining the borough of Retford, in the northern division of the county, hundred of Bassetlaw, union, parliamentary borough, County Court district, petty sessional division, and rural deanery of Retford, No. 1. The parish comprises the village of Clareborough, which is 2 miles from Retford, also the hamlets of Bollam, Welham, Little Gringley, Moorgate, and Spittal Hill, which adjoin Retford, and have been recently added to the Municipal borough. St. John the Baptist's Church at Clareborough was thoroughly restored in 1874, at a cost of £2000, raised by subscription. It was newly roofed and refitted with open benches; a new chamber and organ were erected at the south of the chancel. The church consists of chancel, nave, aisles, south porch, and tower, containing 3 bells. The register dates from 1567. The vicarage is of the annual value of £300, and is in the gift of the trustees of the late Rev. Charles Simeon. There is a Primitive Methodist Chapel. The charities amount to £9 a year. There are several market gardeners here, supplying produce for the Retford and Sheffield markets. The feast is on the 24th of June. Area 3508 acres, rateable value £11,980; population in 1871, 2648.

SCHOOL BOARD.—Mr. W. Clater, chairman; Rev. H. C. Binns, vice-chairman; and Messrs. Stephenson, Chambers, and Hirst. Clerk, Mr. F. W. Wells.

ST. JOHN BAPTIST'S CHURCH.—Services, on Sunday at 10·30, and 2·45; also at 6·30 in three summer months. Sacrament, first Sunday in month. Curate, Rev. H. C. Binns; Churchwardens, Messrs. Thorold and Ogle; Organists, Miss Thorold and Mr. W. Spencer; Parish Clerk, John Thompson. Bickersteth's Hymnal Companion.

PRIMITIVE METHODIST CHAPEL.—Services, Sunday at 6.

POST OFFICE.—John Swinburn, receiver. Letters arrive from Retford at 8, box cleared at 5·30.

The names in Bollam, Moorgate, and Spittal Hill, will be found included in the Retford lists.

Clareborough.

Bingham Mr. William
Binns Rev. Henry Charles, curate, The Parsonage
Booth Miss Mary, dressmaker
Bower John, relieving officer
Hill James, bootmaker
Hutchinson Mr. John Henry, Clareborough hall
Jakes Mrs. Elizabeth, natl schlmstrs
Spencer William, assistant overseer
Stephenson John, wheelwright
Swinburn John, blacksmith
Thompson John, parish clerk
Walker William, miller
Warburton Miss Emma, dressmaker
Warburton Henry, tailor
COTTAGERS.
Gant Henry ‖ Ogle Henry
Spencer Joseph
FARMERS.
Bartle Joseph
Bingley George, Grange farm

Buck Thomas ‖ Dunk Charles
Eaton George ‖ Marriott James
Stamp Richard ‖ Stamp William
Spencer John ‖ Wistow John
MARKET GARDENERS.
Briggs James ‖ Briggs Thomas
Hurst Thomas
Sadler Thomas and Joseph
PUBLICANS.
Chambers Bilby, v, Gate
Foster Mrs. Elizabeth, v, Black Woman
Tinkler Edward, v, King's Arms

Little Gringley.

Baker Robert, v, Plough
Boardman William, shopkeeper
Brewster Alfred, bootmaker
Bland Mrs. Mary, farmer
Bryant George, shopkeeper
Greasby —, tailor
Harrison Thomas, steam cultivator
Hinitt Charles, shopkeeper

Johnson George, cowkeeper
Marr George, tailor's frmn, Balkfield
Millings John, cowkeeper
Rawding William, shopkeeper
Snowden William, shopkeeper
Spencer Henry, seed merchant
Stephenson John, farmer
Ward William, farmer

Welham.

Birks Mr. William, Welham hall
Chappell Mr. William, Welham hm
Clowes George Kenworth, Welham Bridge house
Hutchinson Mrs. Ann
Thorold Charles, Esq, J.P.
Mason James, coal merchant, and r. Hop Pole
Ogle Charles, butcher and grazier
FARMERS.
Bartram John ‖ Hill William
Creighton James, Whinley's farm
Walker George, Whinley's house

White's Directory 1879

48

Clarborough Show

A catalogue of the19th exhibition illustrates the size of the entries.
In all there were 72 classes in the show.

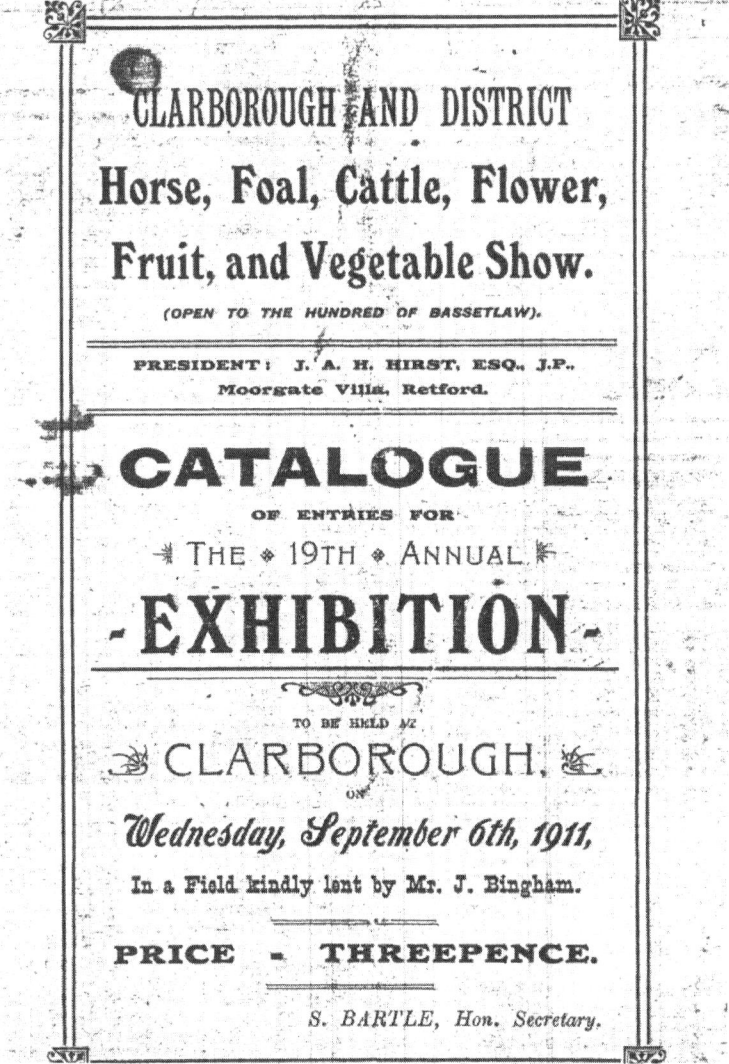

A Selection of photographs of Clarborough show, 1898

Chapter Four

Early Education in Clarborough and Welham

Before 1800 very little provision had been made for the education of poor children as they began work at a very early age. Generally we know that basic literacy was poor. One crude check can be made by seeing how many brides and grooms could sign the marriage register. The Ordsall register from 1830 to 39 shows us that about one third were unable to sign. However, we must remember that more people could read than write.

When we try to research day schools at this time we encounter many difficulties. Some were schools belonging to the parish, supported by a combination of endowments subscriptions and fees, some with, and some without, a connection to the church. Some were private commercial ventures, ranging from fairly conventional elementary schools to an assortment of dame-schools. It has to be said that dame-schools were often considered a place to send the very young, merely to keep them out of trouble and enable the parents to concentrate on their work. The quality of school places varied tremendously and every village appeared to be different.

Research has shown that a Baptist Sunday School was formed at Clarborough in 1830. Each Sunday two teachers made the journey from Retford and plans were made to build a room here. This probably did not materialise for presently it was reported that 'our Sunday school at Clarborough is reduced in numbers....And we now have only 10 scholars'. So the work lapsed. However, whilst it lasted it was extremely well organised: the Superintendents served only for a period of three months at a time and the teachers

– 'of good moral character' – were chosen by ballot. A system of fines was used to keep the staff up to standard. The children had their code of rules also, enforced by the cane when necessary! There was also a system of rewards to help discipline. The school opened at 9.30 and 1.30 every Sunday and a teacher gave each child a text ticket on arrival. Twenty of these could be exchanged for a '20' and counted for a penny towards a prize. Tickets could be forfeited for bad behaviour. There was one dictionary in the schoolroom – of such value one could be fined 1s. for its removal.

The Sunday school seemed to run independently of the Church as rent was paid for the room, coal supplied, as were candles and black lead, copybooks and pencils. One problem with the Sunday schools was that their aim was to teach the children to read the Bible and learn catechisms, but to do this they had to concentrate on basic reading before the religious aspects could be followed. This did not suit some of the religious leaders, who felt the pupils were being distracted from the Bible.

An interesting statement from *The Retford Wesleyan Methodist Sunday School Centenary Booklet* of 1911 gives some insight into what transpired at the Sunday or evening schools in Retford at the time. It comments that the early schools which existed were 'totally insufficient', and that the Sunday and evening schools were needed to help teach the children. In Retford a boys' writing school and a girls' writing school were established which met in the evenings. A fascinating extract discussed the size of candles needed for the evening school and how much coal per year was to be allowed. The candles were placed upon the desks arranged around the walls, the teacher snuffing them now and then in the dim light and keeping an eye on the copybooks. Who knows whether some of the Clarborough and Welham youngsters ventured into Retford of an evening to avail themselves of this opportunity?

Another interesting note in 1823 was to the effect that any pupil absenting himself from the evening school would have to account for himself on the following Sunday where reading and spelling were the order of the day.

Further research shows us that in 1840 there were four dame-schools in Clarborough catering for sixty pupils between them, and one Sunday school containing sixteen boys and twenty-three girls. It was also noted that a Mary Hiley, aged thirty-two and living at the Well House, was a teacher, but where she taught one knows not. The Kelly's Directory of 1848 shows that a John Freeman was a schoolmaster in Clarborough and he is also listed in the White's Directory of 1853. By our next Directory's listing in 1879 the School Board of Clarborough School had been formed.

Strangely enough, it was only the poorest and most destitute children who came within the law, as the Poor Law Amendment Act of 1834 stipulated a minimum of three hours daily instruction in Union Workhouses. At the Retford Union Workhouse fifty year-old Mary Durham had John (thirteen) and Henry (ten) living in with her; she may have been a widow. There were in the 1840s fifteen inmates aged between five and twelve years. Some of the children must have been in the workhouse for fairly brief intervals. Lack of continuity must have been a problem for the teachers, so many did not accept work there.

There was, of course, the King Edward VI Grammar School, East Retford, which was founded in the sixteenth century after a petition from the bailiffs and burgess of East Retford asked for the establishment of a Free Grammar School for the better education of the youths of the parish. The King endowed it with land and East Retford Corporation undertook to make annual payments towards its upkeep. There was an earlier establishment in the fourteenth century and even before, which became defunct as many problems were encountered along the way. A new school, as we know it, was built in 1853 with a tradition based on the Classics, but how many, if any, of the Clarborough and Welham children attended there is open to question, as the pupils were mostly drawn from the middle classes and upper end of the shopkeeper and craftsman groups.

Retford had seven boarding schools in the 1840s and there was one in Moorgate, which of course was in the Clarborough parish in the early years. It was called the Moorgate Ladies' Boarding School, under the direction of the Misses Ward, with a total of twenty-four day and boarding pupils. However, it was not mentioned in the Directory or census of the following year, so one assumes it had closed. Again, how many, if any, from our villages would attend?

In 1840 forty to fifty girls attended the Ladies' Church Sunday School, which was shared jointly by St.Swithun's and St Saviour's in the Clarborough parish. The numbers were small, perhaps because of the hint of exclusiveness contained in its title. There was also a school in Moorgate, associated with St Saviour's, which catered for one hundred and three boys and one hundred and eighty-two girls.

So attempts had been made to educate young people until, finally, in 1870 the Forster Elementary Education Act required Board Schools to be set up to provide elementary education in areas where existing provision was inadequate. The schools remained fee-charging, but poor parents could be exempted.

Clarborough Board School

On 1 May 1871 Ellen Robinson took over the Clarborough Board School with only a monitor for the Infants, a situation of which she did not approve. From this first logbook it is obvious that there were many difficulties to overcome in educating the pupils.

On many occasions the children were away working in the fields. In that first year in July, children were away, haymaking having commenced. In 1875 there was a comment that they were absent tying radishes. In 1880 they were pulling peas and picking potatoes or singling turnips.

In May 1874 many children were away, 'gathering cowslips'. Of course, in those days a long summer school holiday was referred to as the Harvest Holidays, but many families had to engage their children even earlier. The Board used to decide on the length of the Harvest Holiday and in 1889 the head teacher regretted that only three weeks was given, 'as gleaning will not have finished'; so in fact the weeks were extended. In August 1992 the Board decided that the school should only have two weeks' Harvest Holiday, having been previously closed because of an outbreak of measles. As one can imagine, when they returned mid-August, 'the attendance [was] wretched'. It is often recorded, as in January 1990, that 'many children are kept away to go to work who are not eligible to do so'. And in 1895 there was the comment that 'other children are kept at home while their parents go planting'. In 1896 some pupils were employed by market gardeners in July to pick fruit.

An Attendance Officer regularly visited and was given a list of names to check. Sickness was rife and there are many entries listing the number of pupils away. In 1872 '30 children [were] away with flu in January, either themselves or their parents'. In 1875 it was with whooping cough. In 1880 the teacher was 'obliged to send......... home, his face being covered with ringworm'. Ringworm was mentioned also in 1887. In September 1896 two were sent home 'covered with sores'. In 1883 the school was closed in February for two weeks 'in consequence of the children suffering from whooping cough'. Thirty-two had been away ill that week. In July of the same year scarlatina broke out (this is another term for scarlet fever). The school was closed on 9 August for an early beginning to the Harvest Holidays. In November of that year, 'no children who have recovered from scarlatina are allowed to come to school for six weeks by order of the Sanitary Doctor', and the whole school was closed from 3 to 31 December.

In 1904 there was an outbreak of scarlet fever and whooping cough and the school cleaner had to stay away for a month as her children had scarlet fever. The outbreak was so bad that again the school was closed. In 1907 the school was closed for four weeks and the school was then cleaned and whitewashed. In 1908 it was closed early for the Summer holidays because of the mumps.

Individuals occasionally had an even more difficult time. In December 1885 one pupil 'is not to attend school all the Winter, owing to her suffering from a bad throat'.
Other absences, too, were most frequent, with seemingly no reason given. In 1879 there was a comment about one pupil who had 'not been since 1877'. Other entries listed certain pupils who had been absent for six months, or a year. In November 1879, 'two children return to school having been absent since May'. On one occasion the head teacher wrote in dismay that 'Standard Five attend very badly – some days not a child is present'.

The weather also took its toll. In June 1872 '16 children [were] absent owing to the wet'. There are many references to poor attendance when it is snowy or even very cold. In December 1900, 'two children were sent home their feet being wet'. The day had been noted as being very stormy. In 1903 the pupils who had walked two miles to school on a very wet morning were dismissed as they were soaked through – though they then of course had to contemplate the two-mile walk home!

Some pupils had to be sent home because they were dirty. In 1881 in November there is this entry: 'Several children who have been attending school in a dirty state were ordered by the Board to be withdrawn until they were cleaner'. There was one comment that 'the boys' hands are so dirty that they have to be washed two or three times a day'.

On other occasions pupils simply disappeared because the Retford Fair was in town! Eventually the Board began to give a holiday when the Fair was present as in 1894 many pupils 'absented themselves'. In January 1890 '7 boys stayed away from school to go after the hounds, without their parents' consent'. And in 1895 many 'go to the Retford races' without permission.

Consequently, the teacher's task was a hard one, with little continuity amongst the pupils. The lessons taught were quite formal: Reading, Writing, Arithmetic, Grammar, Spelling, Dictation, Recitation, History, Scripture, Singing, and Needlework. Geography was added later. Scripture was very important and the school was visited initially, almost daily, by the Rev. H.C. Binns. Members of the Board also visited most regularly and often supervised or checked the pupils' progress. The school was regularly examined by a Government Inspector, and a Diocesan Inspector, the latter testing their knowledge of the Old and New Testaments, Catechism, Hymns and repetition of some Scriptures. In 1883 the school was informed of the required books to be studied for the year, and the recitation pieces were listed. It is interesting to note that for standard one they had to learn Wordsworth's *To the Cuckoo*, and Standards Five and Six had to learn from Shakespeare's *Merchant of Venice*. In the Infants they had to have an object lesson once a week for half an hour, and three times a week they had appropriate and varied occupations such as threading beads and a ball game.

Gradually the requirements for the Infants became more varied, and in 1889 they enjoyed Embroidery, Sewing and Knitting; Musical Drill was introduced three times a week. In 1892 the sexes were split and while the boys had Drawing the girls had Needlework and Knitting. Drawing appeared to be considered an important subject and in 1892 the boys began to sit a yearly examination in this. In 1896 the results were classed as 'excellent'.

In 1893, in what were termed second-class subjects, the boys in the main school were taught History and the girls Needlework. In 1898 the History period became more specific – The Stuarts. From 1894 onwards the Infants' schedule became even more varied with crayon-drawing and weaving. In 1895 Doll-dressing, Stories and cutting-out were added. It would appear that fiction was not considered initially as in 1890 the list of reading books added to the workbook list were History readers – later, Geography readers were added. It was not until 1896 that the sexes appeared to be treated equally, as then History became one of the lessons for girls as well, and sometimes the sexes worked together instead of girls doing Needlework.

Pupils were formally assessed by the head teacher: at one time she had weekly 'examinations', but much later, in 1905, they became quarterly. In 1887 there was the comment that students should be 'kept down' a year if they had not made sufficient progress. Some too, were to be kept down as they were 'delicate'. In 1896 four 'lazy boys' were kept down. There was an Exceptions Schedule to which pupils were added if they were making poor progress and were not to be examined by the Government Inspector.

The head teacher always commented on the weekly exams and the progress the pupils had made. Progress, as noted by the Inspectors, was varied. In the first Inspector's report in 1872 it stated that 'This school open nine months has already suffered from a change of teacher. The present teacher appears capable and a very fair beginning has been made. Arithmetic and Notation are weak. The order is pleasing'. However, in February 1873 the Inspector noted that 'Unless there are better results in the subject (Arithmetic) the grant will incur a deduction under Article 32 /C1. Eight children are disqualified under article 19/8/1 from bringing any grant to the school'.

And in March 1874: 'I regret to be unable to report any improvements in the work of last year....On the above report my Lords feel compelled to withhold one 10th of the grant for defective instruction....Under this Article a heavier deduction might be incurred another year if no better results were obtained'.
In 1875 1/10 was deducted again. However, in 1877 there was a new head teacher, who had a good inspection.

Payment by results was a distinctly difficult situation for the teacher, bearing in mind our knowledge of frequent absences through agricultural work or illness – or simply deciding not to attend! Consequently in the Log Book entries one can often feel the frustration of the teacher. As early as 1878 there is this comment: 'I find a great difficulty in carrying on the work of the school being without pencils and having so few slates'.

In January 1884 the head teacher discontinues 'home lessons (homework) as so badly done and takes the time of the school', and she later comments that 'the Arithmetic in Standard Three has been

very bad the whole week; not one child had an addition right in the class'. In 1885 she comments that 'the dictation was wretched – 56 errors being made in the class'.
In 1895 the Inspector wrote, rather scathingly, that 'very diligent drilling rather than intelligent teaching is the mark of this school'.

About the Infants was written the following: 'The infants are carefully taught, but there is a singular lack of animation in the teacher, which is reflected in the slow intelligence of the children'.

The head teacher after this obviously took it to heart, as she often mentioned in the Logbook about helping them to be 'brighter and more intelligent'. The Infants were now being kept in the large room with the older pupils most of the time. She begins to mention writing on paper instead of slates, and there was more stress on this. In 1899 the older pupils were working on paper twice a week.

There was frequent concern over the standard of the pupil teachers and monitors. In 1897 the Inspector wrote that 'the pupil teacher should not teach out of the sight of the mistress'. In April 1874 the head teacher was given £3 from the School Committee for teaching and supervising the pupil teacher. In 1879, however, she had been one year and four months without a pupil teacher, and this increased her difficulties. The pupil teacher was given homework by the head as part of her training, took exams locally and in 1904 she had to attend the Grammar School in Retford on alternate Fridays, for training. In 1906 she received Physical Training coaching for pupil teachers, and was taught Modern Methods of the Infant Teacher. Occasionally, as in 1899, one pupil would leave school and would immediately be taken on as a monitor.

We are reminded of the hard work ethos of these times when in September 1901 the monitor had to give up work, 'her services being required at home'. There are many, many comments in the

Log Books of the heads teacher's despair at the poor attendance of the pupils who were desperately needed at home to work in the fields. Another fact noted was the general disposition of the children: in 1889 Friday absences were usually poor, 'many children going home at dinner time and not returning'.

Registers were strictly maintained and in 1899 an Inspector comments, 'Registers should be closed at 1:40pm; they were in the course of being marked at 1.45pm, therefore the attendance must be cancelled'. There was so much concern about poor attendance that in 1908 the managers decided to give a half- day holiday once a month if a certain percentage of attendance was obtained. Following this there was a triumphant entry on one occasion that 96.9% attendance had been recorded!

There was also concern expressed over the poor language of the infants: 'Some are bad talkers and there is great difficulty in making them speak at all'. In 1896 the head comments that the infants had worked well, 'with the exception of two children who cannot talk'.

In 1901 the head's comments suddenly seemed to become happier as regards the state of the pupils' progress. However, this was not how the Inspector viewed the school in March 1902: 'Improvement will be looked for in the teaching of Reading and Geography if the higher grant and the grant under Article 105 of the code are to be continued'. There was the same worry in the 1903 report with the comment that 'the staff must be strengthened if the grant....is to be again claimed'. Sadly, in 1904 they did not receive the higher grant.

An example of how the grant was assessed is shown here. In 1908 the Inspector reported that the pupils were 'stolid and indifferent'.

An Example of a Grant Assessment
(With kind permission of Nottinghamshire Archives)

The Inspectors' reports also covered the general school situation and in June 1903 the report was most uncomplimentary about the rooms being too small, the spouting being broken, the playground needing a new surface, the need for new urinals, and poor drainage. In the 1890 Inspector's Report an extension was proposed for school, as 'the office used by the girls is insufficient in accommodation and unsuitable in structure'. In 1906 a gallery, which used to be in the classroom, was removed.

In June 1903 the school was passed to Nottinghamshire County Council. Matters seemed to improve, and times began to seem more enlightened. In 1907 Voice Production was given ten minutes daily and in 1908 Hygiene lessons were given to the upper Standards every alternate Friday afternoon. The school library was mentioned for the first time in 1908 and then mentioned frequently. Dancing began to be enjoyed in Physical Training lessons and nature walks were first mentioned.

The Diocesan Inspector always gave good reports as the pupils were very well drilled by the visiting clergy.

General discipline, as in most schools, varied according to the time of day, and there are some heartfelt comments on occasion.

In the second month of the school's existence the head writes, 'The little ones have been very tiresome all the day and thrown the whole school in great confusion' - One can imagine!

There were some sad entries. In March 1872 this was noted: 'One little boy away with a broken thigh caused by an engine passing over him as he left school the previous evening'.

In May of that year a pupil dies – we cannot know whether the two entries are linked – and, 'after prayers in the evening the scholars followed the remains of their little schoolfellow to the grave'.

In 1891 there was the sad case of an infant being under police protection as he was being beaten; the Court ordered he had to be taken away from his parents.

There were many happy comments, too. In August of that first year there is the comment that there was a half-day holiday for the tea feast for seventy children, who 'partook of an excellent repast'. There were regular yearly trips for some pupils, for example the Choir trip to Cleethorpes, and a holiday for the Sunday school treat. Royal occasions often occasioned a holiday, as in Jubilee week

1897 when there was a week's holiday as the school was needed 'for dinners and tea' on 22 June. In 1899 the school was closed in March for the Queen's birthday and 'in celebration of the relief of Mafeking'.

There was an interesting description of Empire Day in May 1906 when one of the managers gave an address, and 'patriotic songs were sung, drills were taken in the playground, the Union Jack saluted and each child was presented with a bun, sweets and nuts, which were given by the managers'. Then there was a holiday in the afternoon.

Oranges used to be given to the children before Christmas, and in 1908 children were given money as a Christmas present by the managers. There were frequent days off when the school was used for the one-day Flower Show, or Harvest Festival, a concert or royal marriage, and amusingly, on 8 August 1902 there was a day's holiday 'as market day', and then on 11 August for a Coronation tea for the children.

Only the first forty years of the school's history has been described but one can clearly see the early difficulties and gradual improvement.

In conclusion, one must pay tribute to Frances Searle, who was the headmistress for over thirty years, from 1878 to 1909. What an amazing achievement!

Resources
The Retford Wesleyan Methodist Sunday School Centenary Booklet of 1911
Early Victorian Schools in North Nottinghamshire B.J.Biggs
The Story of the Baptists in Retford and Gamston 1691-1953 J.Hill
The Development of Education in Nottinghamshire 1889-1989
The East Retford National Schools 1813-1858 S>H.Milnes
Gamston Schooling Past and Present
Log Books of Clarborough Board School 1871-1910

Thoughts from Today

Mr Richard Bunn, head teacher from Clarborough Primary School asks the question: is school today so different? The Victorian school mantra of the 3R's – Reading wRiting and aRithmetic – is still at the forefront of education today. The new Primary National Curriculum introduced in September 2014 places these basic skills at its centre, including the presentation of children's work and learning by heart the twelve times table and performance poetry! In fact, I believe there was a fourth R – wRoughting (the skill of Metalwork) to add a further dimension to Victorian education. It is these 4Rs that we see every day in a primary school classroom. The demands of the curriculum require creativity using Design and Technology to express children's ideas.

What has changed? Expectations. The improved teaching pedagogy by highly trained teachers is enabling children to achieve at levels never thought possible thirty years ago, never mind one hundred and thirty years ago! Teachers today, however, are successful for many of the same reasons as their Victorian predecessors – being well-prepared, and having good routines and high expectations of behaviour.

What has changed? The child is now the centre of education; the Victorian teacher delivered a 'one-size-fits-all' education system. I believe that these early formal schools were fundamental in providing the foundations for our modern education system, only the abacus has been replaced by the tablet! These technological innovations have not only raised standards, but also created opportunities to the extent that today's children leaving school will enter the world for careers not yet envisaged or imagined.

The pupils also compared the schooling of Victorian times with that of the present day, describing here, not the village schools, but those in the towns.

Caitlin

In Victorian schools the teachers were very strict and they got angry very easily! If the children were too noisy or didn't get their work done on time they would get whipped by a stick called the cane; the children would get hit also if they had dirty nails or they were very dirty as well. There could be seventy to eighty children in a class and they didn't have very advanced equipment. There weren't any radiators to heat up the room or any paper; instead they used chalk and slates. They didn't have any technology like iPads, laptops or smart boards. The girls were not allowed to wear trousers at all!

In schools today there is lots of technology like laptops, iPads and smart boards. Now we have paper, pencils and pens to use and we have radiators, lights and electricity. The girls today can wear trousers. We have lots of advanced equipment. The ages to go to school are now five to eighteen, unless you are an apprentice and then you can leave school at sixteen. There can be up to about thirty-five in a class nowadays, and the teachers do shout but they don't hit us with a cane. There are mixed classes. Now if we don't get our work done we will be made to finish it the next day but if that doesn't work we do it in break-time sometimes. We don't get into trouble for dirty fingernails now, but we do if we wear nail varnish. Overall, Victorian schools were very different to schools in our day!

Ed

I'm glad that things have changed since Victorian times, especially the schools. Teachers used to put boys in different lessons to the girls because they thought they needed to learn job skills. I am also glad that no schools nowadays separate the girls from the boys. I prefer the technology that helps us to learn. I'm glad we have heating too. They didn't have computers like us and we usually can just go online and find our ancestors. I would type in Ed and there is my family, but Victorians couldn't do that.

Wendy

Hygiene would have been a main priority because your hands would have to be clean all the time or the cane is what you would be whipped with. Teachers believed 'cleanliness is godliness'!

Penny

Victorian children were expected to repeat the answer that the teacher gave them. We now have tables rather than separate desks.

Abbie

In Victorian times they didn't have our technology. Discipline was very harsh: they were hit with a cane, but now all we get is being told off by the teacher.

Sophie

It is different now from then because it isn't sexist. Girls and boys now have equal education. We have much better technology like phones, computers, iPads and even paper! Women can now do whatever job they want because of World War I. It was only after 1870 that children had to go to school.

Nene

In Victorian times children had to go to school from five years old and finish when they were thirteen. And now we go from five to eighteen.

Other comments from seven pupils who chose to be anonymous!

The boys were taught Drawing and Maths because they were thought to have a job involving those subjects. The girls would have Sewing and Cooking because they would one day be a housewife or a dressmaker.

When you got in trouble you would get shouted at and you would get hit by a long hard flexible cane that made you get big warts and blisters all over your hands!

Teachers thought boys should learn skills for jobs. Boys were taught to draw in a precise, technical way.

The classrooms in those days were very cold and old because they didn't have a lot of money to repair the classroom.

If they wanted to write on paper or with a pencil or pen they couldn't because they only had chalkboards, and they sat at desks of two next to someone.

The school was often a church school and was very formal.
I think when you get hit by the cane it must really, really hurt!

Clareborough Church
Nr. Retford

By kind permission of Bassetlaw Museum

Chapter Five
Notable Buildings

The History of St John the Baptist Church, Clarborough

The Domesday Survey of 1086 does not mention a church, but possibly there was one too poorly endowed to be recorded. One had been established by 1103 and part of its income was donated by William of Lovetot to his new Priory in Worksop; then William's son later diverted half of the church's revenues to his family's new monastic enterprises.

Then all goes quiet; possibly it became impoverished and maybe derelict if too much of its income went to Worksop. However, Sewal, Archbishop of York, refounded it in 1258, and the north arcade dates from about this time. Sewal gave the church to the Chapel of St Sepulchre in York, recently built, which needed endowments. He reserved a toft and croft near the churchyard for the vicar, plus the tithes of the enclosed crofts of the town end of the Bolham mills and the altarage. The vicar was responsible for the support of two chaplains to serve at Welham, Bolham and Little Gringley.

In 1393 Clarborough had a Prebendary in York Minster, but we have no details of this nor do we know how the church managed in the religious upheaval of the sixteenth century, except that the impropriation passed to the Crown. Perhaps then it lost its statues and murals and had at least one Puritan vicar. In Henry VIII's reign the first parish registers were started, and the oldest dates from 1567.

Puritanism in the parish affected the Southworth family, and Edward left a small charity endowment to Little Gringley when he fled to Holland with the Pilgrim Fathers. Some years later his widow sailed from Holland to New England and married William

Bradford, second Governor of the new colony. In 1612 Thomas Southworth left behind him 6s. 8d for the payment of tithes, and 20s. 'towards the repairs of the North Causey in Clarborough meadows and the way over Clarborough moor leading from the church to Moorgate'.

Later in the century there was a certain amount of persecution of nonconformists who were mostly Quakers. This was because they failed to take communion in their parish church and pay tithes. One of them, William Hudson of Moorgate, finally secured a licence to hold meetings.

A yew tree was mentioned by Arthur Mee in his book
'Nottinghamshire' (1938) 'Some say the tree is older than the
church and may have been growing a thousand years'
(Photograph by John Sutton, by kind permission of Rev. Mark Cantrill).

Of course, over the years the fabric of the building has been altered. Earlier periods of history are unclear, but nineteenth century changes have been recorded. In about 1825 the interior was renovated, new pews were installed, and a gallery was erected at the west end

A well-known local landowner, H.C. Hutchinson, paid for a small organ to be built in the gallery. The church was thoroughly restored – in some experts' view, over-restored – in 1874 to reflect Victorian tastes. £2000 was raised by subscriptions for re-roofing, for a new organ chamber and instrument on the south side of the chancel, and it was 'refitted with open benches', reducing the number of seats. The ecclesiastical census of 1851 records four hundred seats, whereas an 1895 source mentions two hundred and fifty-nine. The 1851 return describes an afternoon service on 30 March attended by one hundred adults and forty children.

The lychgate was erected in 1897 by Emily Garland in memory of her uncle, William Birks.

At this time St Saviour's, Moorgate, was still in the Clarborough parish and had a thriving attendance at its two Sunday services of seven hundred adults and one hundred and twenty-three children, serving the densely populated section of the growing town.

Clarborough at this time also had Wesleyan and Primitive Methodist Societies with total attendances of over one hundred.

Sources of information: Edna Bradley and W.H.Storrs

Clarborough Public Houses

1830

In Pigot's Directory, The Gate is mentioned; the publican was a John Sherwood. The Red Hart is also mentioned, having a publican called James Pettinger.

1841 Census

There was only one mention of a public house in Clarborough. There was no name recorded but the publican was William Bartle aged twenty-four, his wife Maria aged twenty-three, and son George aged two months.

1851 Census

By the time of the 1851 census there was mention of The Kings Arms and The Black Woman and another public house which is not named and no hint is given about where it was; but in the District 7a details The Gate public house is included.

The publican who ran The Kings Arms was Thomas Barlow of Carlton, recorded as publican and farmer of seventeen acres. He was a widower and lived with his three sons and two daughters.
The publican who ran The Black Woman was a James Stevenson, born at Everton; he was also a wheelwright. His wife was Ann, born in Clarborough: they had six children and a servant named Sarah Storrs, born in Clarborough. On the 1861 census this family lived on Church Lane.

The third public house was run by Joseph Smedley, who lived with his wife and family, three sons and one daughter. Two sons were clog- makers.

1861 Census

In 1861 the census shows that District 8 included The Gate public house but gives no more details.

On Town Street, The Kings Arms was run by William Tinkler aged fifty-five from Leicestershire, with his wife Sarah. He is described as a victualler and farmer of sixteen acres.

The next entry also on Town Street was for The Black Woman, which was run by James Hill aged fifty-eight, a victualler and pig jobber. He lived with his wife Ann and daughter Mary.

Further along Town Street the records show another public house: it is described as The Robin Hood public house and grocer's shop. Charles Richards, aged twenty-four was the publican and grocer. He lived with his wife Hannah and daughter Emma aged less than one month.

1871 Census

The 1871 Census for Clarborough shows no street names or house names, so the only way to trace the public houses is by the occupation of the residents. William Tinkler is stated to be a farmer living with his wife Sarah, and son Edward, who is described as a publican, his wife Annie, brother Frank and grandson William (Edward and Annie's son) aged three months. We presume that this is The Kings Arms as William was publican in the 1861 census.

The only other record is for a George Foster, aged thirty-two from Whitwell, and recorded as an innkeeper. He was living here with his wife Elizabeth and daughters Mary Ann aged two, and Fanny aged two months. This public house is probably The Black Woman. There is no record of The Gate but it is still named on the district description.

1881 Census

On the 1881 census at the Gate is Bilby Chambers, born at Hayton, innkeeper, and his family of six sons and two daughters. This included a son and father-in-law who were boatmen.

Edward Tinkler, widower, was at The Kings Arms and is stated to be a publican and farmer. Also here were Albert Tinkler, son, aged eight years, Sarah, Edward's mother, aged eighty-five years, and Elizabeth Storrs, aged thirty-eight years, who was a housekeeper.
The Black Woman has George Otter, born in Dunham, as the innkeeper, along with his wife Agnes, son Charlton and daughters Mary E. and Millicent.

1891 Census

The Gate Inn was the first mentioned on this census and had Bilby Chambers as innkeeper and boatman, with his family of four sons and two daughters.

In this census, The Black Woman has George Otter as the innkeeper, with his wife Agnes and daughter Agnes.

The Kings Arms still has Edward Tinkler as the innkeeper, with Albert his son and Elizabeth Storrs as servant.

1901 Census

The Kings Arms still had Edward Tinkler as a farmer and publican, Albert his son as a general labourer working from home and Elizabeth Storrs as housekeeper.
Further along the village street at The Black Woman was Thomas Mills, who was born in Mattersey, his wife Emily, son John Thomas and daughter Emily Ethel.
The Gate still had Bilby Chambers as publican and road-man with his wife Hannah, sons John, a saddler, and William and granddaughter Millie Nelly Bartle, who was also a boatman.

1911 Census
The Kings Arms had Bilby Chambers aged seventy-five, previously of The Gate Inn, his wife Hannah aged seventy, granddaughter Nellie, now Bartram, Samuel Bartram and children Harry and Mary Frances living with them. Bilby was a publican and roadman for U.D.C.

The publican of The Black Woman was John Surgey, living with his wife Anne, three sons and a servant named Annie Riley.

John Hague, from Bradfield near Sheffield, was the publican of The Gate Inn. Also living here was his son Alonzo, wife Emily and granddaughter.

Research by Barbara Swannack, December 2014

The Clarborough Workhouse

There had been houses for the destitute in Retford, Thrumpton and Moorgate previously, but in 1818 a Workhouse was built in Grove Street at a cost of a thousand pounds. The poor of twenty-six surrounding parishes could be sent there, each parish contributing £3 per annum + 3s. per week for each person sent. Conditions were harsh, and an example of this is when in 1821 it was ordered at the Meeting of the Moot Hall that the walls adjoining the Workhouse Yard be raised so much as may be necessary to prevent paupers from escaping!

It should be noted here that at this time the Clarborough parish geographically extended nearly into Retford and became more centralised to the village only in 1934.

The second Workhouse, the East Retford Workhouse, based in the Clarborough parish, was opened in 1838 as a result of the new Poor Law Amendment Act. The administration was no longer to be under the individual parish but a union of parishes, and on a much larger scale, capable of maintaining two hundred paupers and governed by a Board of fifty-two Guardians under a Committee which was then responsible to the Poor Law Commissioners in London. The first proposed site was in Ordsall, but this contract was never concluded, and the new site in the Clarborough parish was at the top of Spital Hill. It was a three-storey building, the plan of which revealed three spoke wheels radiating from a central hub where the Master had his quarters and a dominant view of the spokes. It seems the Workhouse was never filled to capacity and was generally two thirds full. The 1860s reference books inform us that on average only seventy-two were inside, which indicates a certain prosperity in the area at that time, and of course, the discouraging effects of Workhouse life on paupers. It was the most

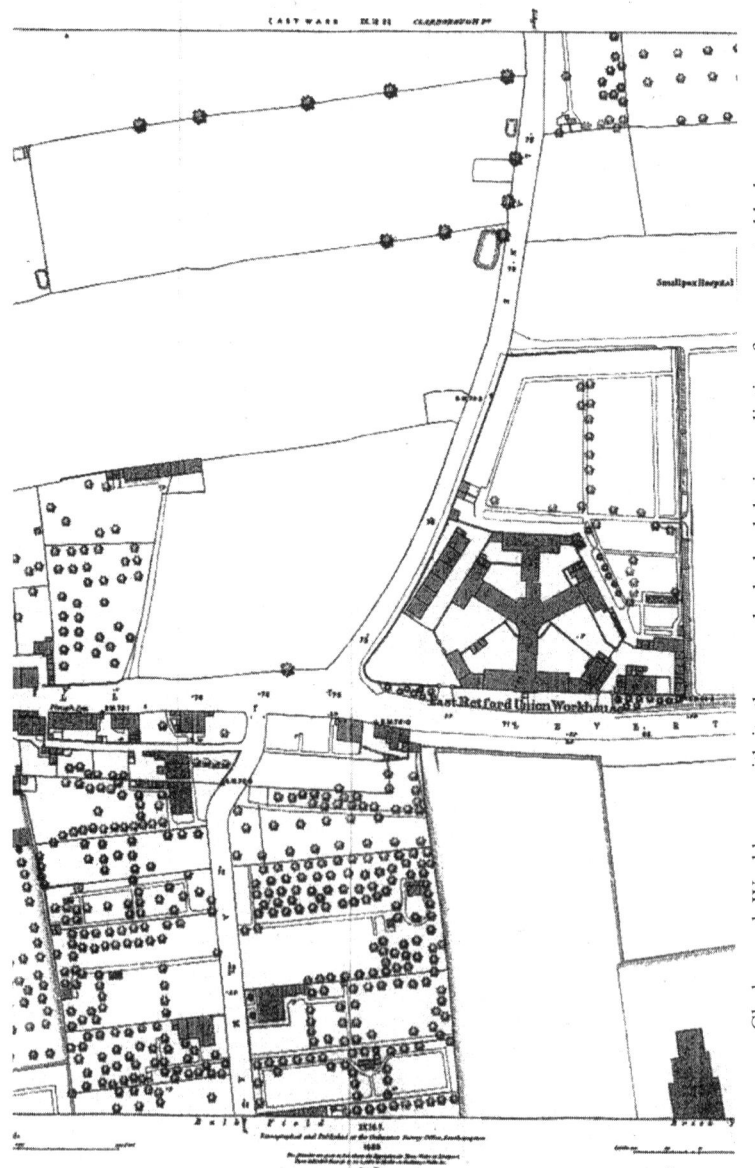

Clarborough Workhouse with its three-spoked wheel design radiating from a central hub.

(With kind Permission of Bassetlaw Museum)

hated and depressing place. In the 1881 census eighty-seven inmates were recorded, from a one month-old baby to an eighty-three year-old. One family had four children with them, and the census uses terms like 'lunatic', 'imbecile' and 'idiot' which were not meant to be derogatory but merely the terms that were used at that time.

The Workhouse, Spital Hill. Photo taken about 1910.
(With kind permission of Bassetlaw Museum)

Prices are always interesting and the new building was costed at £2872 but finally cost £4500. While the building was progressing the Union maintained three existing workhouses in Tuxford, Retford and Clarborough, which received paupers from parishes outside the boundaries of the new Union. In March 1837 they were told to accept no further admissions, although the Clarborough one in Moorgate continued to until 1838. After this date all paupers within the parishes of the Union were sent to the East Retford Workhouse and each parish contributed a certain amount towards its maintenance depending upon the average number of paupers sent from their parish to the Workhouse every three years. The total cost of the Workhouse was charged to the parishes of the Union as Poor Rate, although some received a contribution when the old Moorgate Workhouse was sold for £87.10s. In January 1839 the Tuxford Workhouse was sold for £206.

The first Master and Matron were a Joseph Cheatter and his wife, aged sixty-seven, at a salary of £60 per annum with free accommodation and stated weekly rations. Details of the furnishings, heating and ventilation were decided by the Guardians, and details were most precise, with for example, one peck of coal being allowed each day for every ward with a fireplace.

It appears from some of the detail available that the Clarborough Workhouse was not as harsh as some in separating families, as there were plans to fit out a workroom as dormitories for married tenants. However, in contradiction, a fence with gates was erected to ensure there was no communication between the sexes between the two sides of the building. This was not altogether effective as various inmates managed to circumnavigate the rule and a bastard child was delivered of an inmate in 1850!

Under the 1834 Act, the old, the young, the insane and the sane were to be housed and cared for separately, but there is no indication that this happened in Retford as there was one incident where a resident was taken before the magistrates for assaulting an 'idiot' pauper.

From records it would appear that keeping the School Master and Mistress proved difficult and at one point the Porter took over the office as well as his other duties and was given a salary of £10 per year in addition to the personal allowances which he received as a Porter. The Master and Matron, Schoolmaster and Porter made up the entire staff of the Workhouse plus the Chaplain. Before the Chaplain was appointed, the Master and Matron had to conduct the paupers to church every Sunday, either to St Saviour's or to East Retford, depending on where a service was held. Those who had Workhouse duties in the morning had to attend either in the afternoon or evening.

In Retford it was first decided in March 1837 that no pauper residing out of the Union would be entitled to relief, but in March 1845 it was agreed that each Union should be responsible for its poor whether resident in, or out of, the Union.

Some relief was given out of the Workhouse, such as assisting pauper families to emigrate, or providing bread for the poor. On occasions warrants for the arrest of men who had deserted their families were also granted.

The Retford Workhouse appeared more benevolent than some, as children were educated and adequately clothed. Although the children were supposed to go to school, this sometimes did not happen as some of the older girls had to look after the younger children at this time, as the Schoolmistress had too many children to cope with. Some boys were apprenticed, for example one to a weaver and four recommended for light work. Besides school they could exercise in the exercise yard and were allowed to be accompanied into town for half an hour, but segregated – boys one way and girls the other!

The able-bodied were expected to work, and during the building of the house some had been employed in breaking stones and making roads connected with the house for 3d a day, and this continued after the Workhouse had been built. It was a much-hated job. The Guardians would have boulder-sized stone delivered to the Workhouse, where it was broken down and sold to the parishes of the Borough Council for road- mending. The Workhouse hoped to be self-sufficient and endeavoured to grow its own vegetables as far as possible. The women were employed in household duties and the Guardians decided that bread for out-relief distribution should be baked in the Workhouse. It is thought that casual wards were built away from the main building where casuals could have a bed, bath and breakfast and food in return for breaking stones.

Discipline was strict. A pauper was allowed to leave the premises, with permission, perhaps to visit a near relative who was ill, or attend a funeral, but if he did not return on time he forfeited his place in the Workhouse. Occasionally leave might be allowed if someone wished to look for work. Sometimes inmates absconded and when found were punished. Confinement and a drastically reduced diet was the usual punishment.

The diet was basic with bread and potatoes a staple part, with limited protein, dairy and meat. Potatoes were grown on the premises and rice occasionally used as a substitute. Vegetables were also grown. It would appear from research that different allowances were given to various age groups. For medical reasons there are records of sulphur being mixed with treacle to give to the children to prevent the 'itch', a colloquial term used for scabies. Brimstone is a common name for sulphur and was supposed to rid the body of this condition. They did have an isolation hospital in the grounds for serious cases, but these were not common. They realised that dirt bred disease and acted accordingly. In January 1839 all children coming into the Workhouse were vaccinated against smallpox.

Guards of the German prisoners of war held at the workhouse.

Taken between 1914-18

(by kind permission of Bassetlaw Museum)

In the 1930s the building was taken over by the County Council and became an old people's home, Hillcrest Hospital, which closed in 1972. Bassetlaw Museum has details of when, in the First World War, the Workhouse was taken over in order to house German prisoners of war.

It is thought by some that the post box at the corner of Lidget Lane and Leverton Road is in fact all that remains of the original brickwork of the old Workhouse. Has any reader any knowledge concerning this?

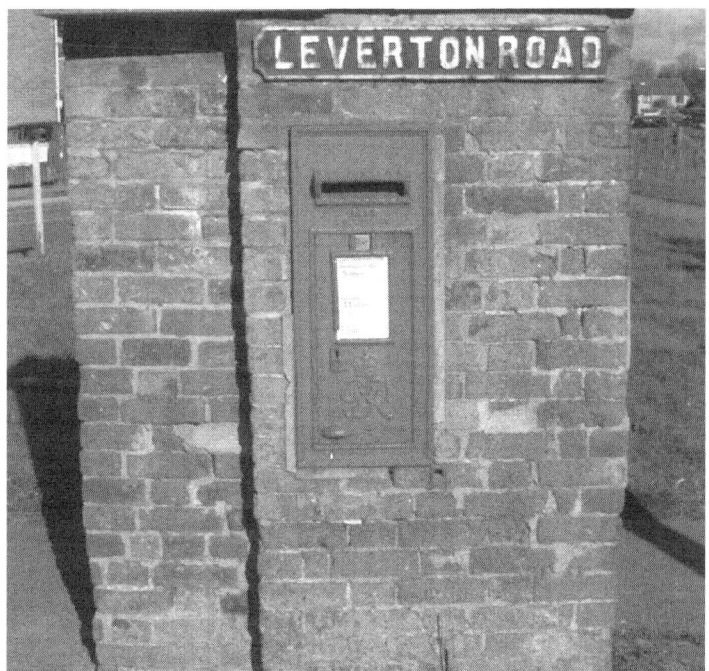

The post-box with, possibly, the original brickwork from the workhouse.
(Photo by John Sutton)

Resources
The Book of Retford J.Roffey
The Early Days of Retford Workhouse Dorinda Clark
History of Retford Jackson

Where is the Well in Welham?

According to several articles that I have managed to obtain, it is here at our house, 'Well House', in what is now Bonemill Lane, formerly Well House Lane. Undoubtedly the original part of the house is the Spa that was built by John Hutchinson in the early 1700s. Arthur Mee in *The King's England Nottinghamshire* in 1938 writes that 'below the floor of a cottage on the lane to Welham is the once-renowned well which gave that village its name. A flight of steps goes down to the water in a stone basin 12 ft. square'. I am sure that many of the residents aged over forty and still living here will be able to confirm this following the school outings that used to visit here.

John Piercy wrote in 1828 in *The History of Retford in the County of Nottingham* as follows: 'Welham, or the Hamlet of the Well, is supposed to have derived its name from the once-celebrated spring St John's Well near the place, which was formed into a large bath, and still remains entire. During the early part of last century, it was famous for many cures, but latterly it has lost much of its celebrity. The late John Hutchinson Esq. erected a cottage adjoining and enclosed the bath to preserve it from injury. Here was, until lately a feast or fair, held annually on St John's day, to which the neighbouring villagers resorted to enjoy such rural sports as fancy might dictate. Cold baths like this were formally regarded with superstitious reverence, being supposed to possess a sovereign remedy for agues, rheumatism etc.'(Probably, they were also welcome after the flights of fancy!)

I would like to thank local historian Ross Parish for giving me the above references during his research visit. Other items that emerged during my research work were that Arthur Robert Garland of Welham Hall purchased from the 'deceased estate' of John Henry Hutchinson of Clarborough Hall acres 117.3.16 along with

86

Well House Cottage and garden for the sum of £3200 on 16 October 1910. He then sold the cottage and garden to Fred Anderson on 5 November 1910 for £130. This was subsequently bought by the late Mr Eric Durham on 14 October 1955, later to be purchased by me on 27 March 1975.

Further articles in the *Retford Times* on 14 June 1957 and 2 July 1970 give much of the above information along with the other points of interest. The Domesday Book refers to Wellun (at the spring); this had changed to Wellum by 1166 and by the sixteenth century had become Wellom, but in Chapman and Andres's map of Nottinghamshire in 1775 it was shown as Welham. By 1830 the spring had lost much of its popularity as people became able to travel to the warmer (but no more effective) spas. The water was originally taken internally and, indeed, prior to mains water in 1938, served as the water source for the local farms and cottages. One such house was Hop Field Cottage where hops were grown for maltings. Hops can still be found in the local hedgerows including here at Well House.

The smaller building is the well-house (now a kitchen). Under the floor is the bath. (Photo by John Sutton by kind permission of Glynn and Jenny Whelan)

The bath is now below the kitchen and is entered via a trapdoor.
The brick walls can be seen with water below - often two feet deep!
(Photo with kind permission of Jenny and Glyn Whelan)

The secret behind the power of the water is its very high mineral content as it soaks through the gypsum in Clarborough hills. It is drinkable, but only in small quantities, as it is very high in magnesium and sulphate, the predominate ingredients of Andrews Liver Salts. It is quite chalky to taste and flat, but is very pleasant to drink if aerated.

Other tales we have been able to glean from locals are that the lane used to be virtually a tunnel as the hedgerows joined above. Also it is believed that a vicar of Babworth died of a heart attack while taking the very cold water. We would very much appreciate any further information that any readers are able to give us.

The spring today is diverted round the house and can be seen pouring out into the dyke halfway down our garden. It is still very prolific at several gallons per minute; this does not reduce even in the driest summers.

Glynn and Jenny Whelan

Bone Mill Farm

As was discovered in discussion with the present owners of Bone Mill Farm, Jeff and Jacque Williamson, the farm has quite a history.

After the canal was built in 1777 the Bone Mill was erected where bones were brought and fed into a hole in the wall. There is evidence in the beams of the Bone Mill roof of gear wheels, which Jeff has been told were worked by horses walking round in a circle outside. This worked the process whereby the bones were then ground between stones, some of which are still in the garden. Then the bone meal was taken by canal to be used as either fertiliser or as an addition to cattle food.

Showing the roof structure of the Bone Mill
(Photo by John Sutton by kind permission of Jacque and Jeff Williamson)

The Bone Mill

Photo by John Sutton by kind permission of Jeff and Jacque Williamson

One of the grinding stones

(Photo by John Sutton by kind permission of Jeff and Jacque Williamson)

In the Bone Mill there are some original beams, which are all held in place by wooden pegs. Some beams are thirty feet long. The marks used to match the joint together can be seen. This photo shows the builders' marks where beams are to match.

(Photo by John Sutton with kind permission of Jeff and Jacque Williamson)

The house was built onto the Bone Mill later, possibly as additions on separate occasions, and certainly one addition is noted in stone as 1828. Jeff has extended a great deal of it, and here again one can see original beams which are pegged, and arched windows in the old brick walls. In the lounge Jeff has used the original bricks from the floor of the Bone Mill, and a beam from Clarborough church, which he bought when a new belfry was installed, to form his new chimneybreast.

It would be so interesting to find out more about this historic building.

Chapter Five

Reminiscences of the Villagers

Chris Boothby

Chris has lived in Clarborough all his life and his present home down Big Lane was bought by his father from the Chambers family, who have given Chris some photographs, one of which has been printed here.

Mrs Chambers when she was young, taken around 1925 outside
Plum Tree Cottage. (Photo by kind permission of Chris and Kathryn Boothby)

Just recently Chris spoke to a young man who was researching his family tree, who stated that in the past Big Lane used to be known as Briggs Lane because of two Briggs brothers who built both Celery Cottage and Chris's own Plumtree Cottage. The cottages date back to 1785 or thereabouts.

When Chris was young, on the Main Street lived the Stevensons next to the joiner's shop, and the Tunstalls lived in a little cottage next to them. Chris was born in a cottage on the Main Street set back quite a way from the road and is now called Sickle Brook. In one part of the semi-detached house lived Rosalie Dunstan and next door was where Chris lived. It was located so far back that the end of the garden would have been at the bottom left-hand corner of the garden at Stanford House now. He remembers making a hole in the hedge and cutting through to school through the fields which was much quicker than following the main roads. Mrs Allen was his head teacher and he remembers Mrs Hunter, who taught in the smaller of the two rooms. He remembers the children's coat- pegs and using chalk on the blackboard.

As a young boy he attended Sunday School and recalls the delights of the yearly trip to Cleethorpes, often driven in a bus by George Hird from Clayworth – the sort of old bus now sometimes seen outside the Bassetlaw Museum on gala days! They used to stop at a pub at Bishops Bridge on the way for pop and crisps and the same on the way back. As you got on the bus you were greeted by a thick fug of smoke as George enjoyed his cigar!

One of his childhood memories concerns his brother and Peter Taylor, who lived in one of the two cottages down Church Lane, now Stanford House, who used to hold Punch and Judy shows in one of the brick buildings in Michael Baines's yard. One building had an open end for the cattle in winter and there they used to place benches on some Sundays, and charge the children. We're talking some sixty-five years ago now!

Another memory concerns the Coronation crown which every child received from Lady Bailey who lived at Clarborough Hall.

Chris was a Cub Scout and the meetings were taken by the vicar of Clarborough and Hayton, a Rev Martin, at the Hayton vicarage, which had extensive grounds. Here they used to make fires and camp out. The entrance to the vicarage was down the lane in

Hayton where there are now bungalows – Peter Eames's being the corner one. At that time it was very wooded. One really amusing incident Chris recalls is when the vicar one evening was trying to teach them First Aid and how one should try to resuscitate the patient. The vicar, evidently as a demonstration, lay down on the floor and began to undo his shirt buttons, so a member of the Cubs leapt forward to help him but perhaps was too enthusiastic in his disrobing!

How places have changed is always fascinating and Chris describes how Howbeck Lane used to be referred to as Blaggs Lane – perhaps a Blaggs family were well known there? At the corner of Howbeck where Howbeck House is now, there used to be a farm owned by the Burtons, then before them the Hethershaws and the Starrs.

Chris fondly remembers Mrs Hird's sweetshop before it became the fish shop owned by Mrs Bundy, and skating on the pond at the corner of Church Lane. He recollects a wooden green caravan-type structure which used to be on the left-hand side down Big Lane where at one time a Johnny Whitlam lived. He also remembers a couple called Charlie and Freda who, when he was about ten years old, lived down Barcroft Lane in an old bus. Charlie worked on the canals and Freda used to push her Silver Cross pram on her way to the shops, smoking a cigarette with its ever-growing tip of ash! He remembers the size of the Clarborough Workhouse up Spital Hill. Chris also recollects how popular this area was for Sheffield folk who used to come here for the fishing at the weekend, and some of them returned to live here. He remembers many years ago someone saying that sewage from Sheffield used to be brought to the Welham railway sidings and spread on the land here.

Edna Bradley (nee Durham)

Edna Bradley has always lived in Clarborough and was born down Bone Mill Lane. We have mention of her christening in a book kept by Mr Stevenson the Clerk and Sexton to the Clarborough Parish Church from 1894. On this page is the date of Edna's christening which was November 11 November 1923. Interestingly, on the same page, was the christening of her future husband William Bradley on 23 September 23 1923.

Numbers 189&190 show the christenings of William Bradley and Edna Durham who later married. (Reproduced by kind permission of Judith Gourley)

Edna attended the village school and remembers two teachers, Nelly and May Thorpe, who used to live at Little Gringley.

Pupils of Clarborough School 1935, the year of King George V and
Queen Mary's Silver Jubilee. Edna is 5th from right on second row.
(Photo by kind permission of Edna Bradley)

The villages, of course, were vastly different then. She attended
school and church but did not feel really connected to the villages,
living as she did at a distance. School seemed a long way away and
she walked with her older sister and younger brother. She
remembers the races they used to enjoy on special occasions in the
field next to school.

Church was a very important part of her life and she attended three
times on Sunday – the Morning Service, Sunday school in the
afternoon, and then the Evening Service. You always had to be
dressed in your best, so it was white socks, pretty dress and a straw
hat. She was asked to join the choir in her later years at
Clarborough School and remembers the choir practices every
Friday with Harry Blagg, the choirmaster and organist. They sang
twice every Sunday and there were four rows in the choir – men,
women, girls and boys. Mr Stevenson, the Sexton, used to light the
oil lamps and the church always appeared warm because of the

boiler in the basement. Church festivals such as the Harvest Festival were remembered fondly, with the Church full of the farmers and their produce, which used to be taken to the Retford Hospital, which at that time was an in-patient hospital. The Patronal Festival in June was celebrated as a Flower Service with eggs, and these too were taken to the hospital.

Edna remembers the joiner's shop at the top of Church Lane and the many fields where now the houses and bungalows stand. Dances were popular at the Village Institute, a wooden building with a wooden floor. She recollects that they enjoyed live music on many occasions.

Edna first knew her future husband at school, and when they first married they lived in one of the two cottages down Church Lane for a year before moving to a property down Big Lane. Then later they moved to Orchard House in 1967.

When the war started the Church Choir broke up and did not reorganise for many years. The latest service was at 3 pm because of the blackout and there being no lights. Edna remembers there were no air raid shelters, as the area was so rural no bombing was expected, although they could hear the bombs falling in Sheffield, and one did land near the Tunnel.

I am grateful for her notes on the History of Clarborough Church, which contain items not mentioned in the history books I have read. These notes are printed elsewhere.

Edna was able to provide some fascinating photographs. The first one, of the pupils at Clarborough School in 1901, shows her mother, fourth from the right on the front row, clutching her pinafore.

The second one was taken at the Clarborough Show in 1910; this shows how important and busy an occasion it was. Edna's grandfather is thought to be on the second row, fifth from the left. He was George Baines, a farmer who lived at Hilltop Farm.

Edna has given us more insight into Clarborough and Welham's past.

Ann and Louis Cobb, Rosetta Gleaden (nee Cobb) and Janet Freeborough (nee Jackson)

Rosetta, Louis and Janet are all cousins and with Ann remembered many happy times in their early life in Clarborough. There was a great community spirit and everyone worked and played together.

The Cobb family goes back many, many years and were in Hayton from 1662 until they moved to Clarborough in 1901. They are linked to the Ogle family. Louis and Rosetta lived next door to Granny Cobb's smallholding where Baulk House is now. Their cottage was part of the old Premier Garage Site, and they were both born there, with one brother and one sister. They then moved to South View Farm, which was a lovely large farm with a seventeen-bay Dutch barn attached to it and paddocks which went down to the canal. Here the third sister, Marian, was born.

South View Farm in 1950s. You can see the children playing in the garden at one of Rosetta's birthday parties.
(Photo by kind permission of Rosetta Gleadon)

Nottingham County Council compulsorily purchased part of the land to build Clarborough Junior School and the rest then was sold for development. Then the family moved to Manor Farm, Hayton.

South View Farm gave them a carefree childhood and there were fond memories of playing on a huge inner tube from an aeroplane; this was kept on their lawn and many village children bounced and played on it. Village sports were held in fields there.

The village had a week of celebrations for the Festival of Britain in 1951 and one of the events was a parade where they went round Retford on three tractors and trailers. Rosetta dressed as Bo Peep. Rosetta's mum hired the costumes from Preston's, at the corner of the Market Square in Retford. Evidently the shop also sold ice cream.

Festival of Britain Parade 1951
From left to right: Ruth White, Carols White, David Howard, Doreen Jackson, Lucy Jackson, Jennifer Thorley, Peter Thorley,?,Rosetta Cobb, Angela Rice, Elizabeth Hill, Dennis Heathershaw, Jack Elson (driver), Mr Thoreby
(by kind permission of Stella and Lewis Taylor)

They enjoyed the Youth Club, run by Mr Jones, the head of the village school who was remembered with the greatest respect. Rosetta recalls him taking them all to London to a TV centre where they were recording a Peggy Mount comedy. Youth Club Members were quite shocked to realise that there was no spontaneity from the audience and that they were told when to applaud or laugh! Mr Jones filmed the trip and it was a wonderful experience for them.

Like Ruth Hunter, Rosetta remembers that you had to attend the Sunday evening service before you could attend the Sunday evening Youth Club. On other occasions it was held in the Village Institute. Everyone was sad when Mr Jones left, as he was an enthusiastic person who was very fair and well respected.

They used to play on tennis courts, which were on the left just before the curve of Clarborough Hill. There were regular dances at the Village Institute, sometimes with live bands before they became too expensive. Rosetta's father bought a radiogram from Henry Spencer's salesroom, and he used it when he was MC at the Institute. Sometimes Bennett's milk trolley was used to take the radiogram to the Village Institute.

The Institute was the hub of the village and the committee used to work really hard. On Sports Day there was either a sit-down tea, or a picnic in a bag, which was provided to everyone. After Sports Day, at the evening dance, your name was called out to get your prize and Rosetta thinks that her love of bunting – much of which she has made recently – comes from her happy childhood memories when bunting was often present.
A bar was built in the Village Institute by Grandad Cobb, and Dick Baker helped.

Discipline was strict in those days, and there was more respect for others. The local policeman could give you a cuff and no one objected. In fact you didn't tell your parents or else you would receive another one!

Harvest Supper at the Institute was well remembered, and Rosetta recalls rabbit pie being made at Howards in Retford, for the supper. There was also a Whitsuntide Egg-and-Flowers Service, when you collected eggs in a decorated basket and met in school first. The contents were distributed to the local hospital with some of the market gardeners' produce also. Sunday School trips to Cleethorpes were happily remembered.

Their father owned a boat called Merlin on which the children played. On one occasion Jean Baker toppled over in her pretty yellow dress and fell into the canal.

There were no houses down the left of the Smeath and they recalled playing in the fields. Skating in Winter was a favourite pastime at Church Lane Corner. Riding the donkeys, too, was enjoyed, from South View Farm right around the fields and back. Rosetta's father used to look after the donkeys in Winter for a gentleman from Mablethorpe.

Some of the characters from the village were recalled. Mr Shuttleworth lived in a cottage on the Main Street and used to offer you a peppermint balanced on a piece of cardboard. Mrs Bundy owned the fish-and-chip shop and Rosetta was the first customer! Mr Wardhaugh owned the village shop and was well known for his trick of making a coin disappear. They sold Wall's ice cream on a Sunday and it was a great treat. Janet used to work at the village shop.

Mrs Oxley owned a Rolls Royce and kindly gave gifts to the schoolchildren at Christmas, which tradition Rosetta and Louis's parents continued. Mrs Oxley had a chauffeur and lived at Welham

Park. Mrs Jeffcock lived where Richard Kay now lives and was also a benefactor to the village school.

Mr Baines's house, which is Manor Farm, was the venue of an amusing incident when the children were playing together nearby. The ball went in and broke one of the windows at the back of the house and the children were very concerned. Louis's mother had a handyman who neatly repaired the tiny pane but they realised that in fact all the glass from the window had gone into the house and so therefore the incident would be noticed on Mr Baines's return. However, it was never mentioned and none of the children got into trouble, possibly because the housekeeper cleaned it up!

Mr Dunstan was remembered because as he passed Manor Farm he used to take a buttonhole from one of the rose bushes; in fact this rose bush is thought to be many years old.

Much conversation then took place about the visitors to the village, such as the scissor-grinder, the fish man, and the Baker brothers who used to bring warm hot cross buns. The butcher used to come and Ann remembers going out with a really big plate and returning with it full of meat. Markhams from Gainsborough delivered pop and ginger beer in stone jars and a Mr Thurman from Retford used to come with two great suitcases and go round the houses selling his goods.

Louis described when deep drainage came to the village. The spoil from it went into a hollow, which was called Clarks Yard Field; it was eventually smoothed over and three bungalows were built on it on the Main Street.

They recalled some of the sad happenings in the village. One was when Jack Elsom was killed: after alighting from the 10.30 bus and walking at the back of the bus, he was then hit by a vehicle.

Another was when the local policeman, Steve Atkinson, was killed as he was helping a local farmer to load up his beasts outside Jillian's cottage on the main road in Welham and was also hit by a vehicle.

Janet and her two friends, Janet Boothby and Edith Jackson, had an amazing escape one morning as they were waiting at 8:30 am to catch Hurton's school bus to Hallcroft School. The snow was really high and a lorry had overturned in the field at the end of Barcroft Lane with its wheels in the air. The girls walked up from the bus stop to have a look and a petrol tanker then came down the hill, hit the curb in passing, then spun and threw them into the dyke. Janet was in shock, but did not tell her mother at first what had happened; she simply went home and said she felt unwell. She thought one of them might have continued on to school. Later BP came and saw them all and gave them some money.

They remember two incidents concerning the cottages on the right as you begin to drive up Clarborough Hill. Both on different occasions were hit by lorries. Roy Abbot's cottage was hit with an impact so great that all the bricks of the gable end came out and the bedroom upstairs was exposed and you could see the bed. Rose Cottage was due to be signed over to a young couple that day, but the deal, in fact, still went through.

They have very vivid memories of their families, of course. Granny Cobb used to churn her own butter and the churn still sits in Ann and Louis's entrance. Louis's arm used to ache after turning the handle! Granny also used to sell petrol and as she waited for customers she used to peg rugs with Readicut. She then gave them away for prizes at the Church sales. The Harvest sales were in the Chapel and were well attended.

Louis and Rosetta's parents were very involved in village life and very generous. Fred used to deliver free coal to the pensioners on Christmas Day, and in fact this generosity almost got him into trouble as the police claimed he hadn't a licence for his lorry for such an activity. When he rescued the schoolchildren from flooding by collecting them from the school and transporting them into the village with his lorry, this too caused the police to comment!

Janet was born at Meadow Farm down Bone Mill Lane, along with her two sisters; now it is the Hogg's farm. She described how the fishermen came in droves at the weekend to fish. Her mother used to make them tea. They brought their own tea and sugar and she used to mash it and give them the milk for 6d. There was a two-shilling deposit when they collected the crockery, which of course was given them back on its return.

The fishermen brought all their families from Sheffield and her father, who was a market gardener, used to sell them produce. Other smallholders too, used to sell their goods. Rosetta remembers ten to twelve busloads of fishermen parking at the bottom of Clarborough Hill and down Smeath Lane, where they could then go and fish on the Chesterfield Canal.

They all agreed that the move to a secondary school in Retford was a huge change after their time at the village school, which was remembered for its coal fires, frozen milk and the stove in the hall, which once blew up! Louis used to watch the hands of the big clock, as the time passed so slowly! He remembers a friend arriving at school with some cordite and dropping it into the inkwell and stating that he was going to blow up the school! Janet recalls that you were taken to school only on the first day, and then expected to walk thereafter by yourself, and what a shock it was to walk such a long way.

Rosetta and her friend were horrified when they first encountered the terrifying PE equipment at the Hallcroft School, of climbing ropes and the vaulting box, such a shock after using only simple equipment at the village school. On viewing the vaulting box her friend whispered, ' What do we do with that – get inside it?' This led to reminiscences of the habits of old: how one used to make ginger beer at home and hear the corks as they popped out; drinking cowslip wine was supposed to bring the spots out in measles; a bunch of young nettles was sometimes eaten as 'spinach'.

The Lane Letting Book
(Photo by John Sutton)

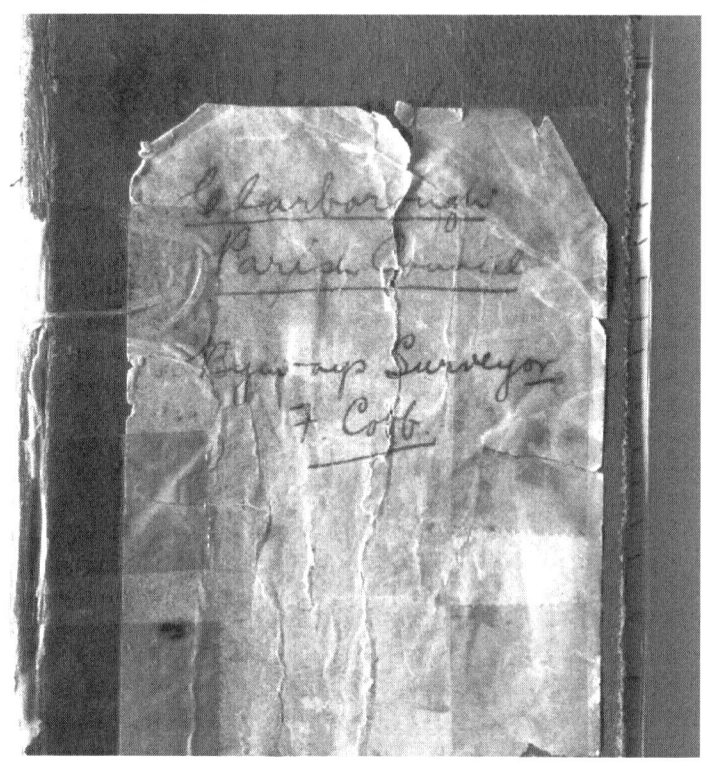

The Lane Letting Book
(by kind permission of Clarborough and
Welham Council. Photo by John Sutton)

Louis was able to describe 'Lane letting' to me. It is mentioned in both the Inclosure Act and the Minutes. It was the sides of the lane that were let for cattle grazing. Children used to say that they were 'tenting' or 'tenting cattle', meaning that they were looking after the cattle and then staying with them just for a couple of hours before they took them back home. Research shows that 'tenting' is a Middle English word derived from the Latin word 'attendita', meaning to wait or attend. - Life is so different now!

Thelma Cooke

Shortly after we moved into the Old Vicarage on Church Lane, we invited the previous owners for a meal. The conversation came round to ghosts. I asked if in fact we had one and the reply was – YES! This confirmed our suspicions, because at a certain spot on the back landing there is a chill and all the hairs on the back of your neck stand up. We also told them about our daughter having seen a little girl in her bedroom and she described what she had seen. The girl was dressed in a nightdress with a border of lace and had long hair, and as our daughter was looking at her she faded away.

The guests then told us the Old Vicarage used to be a farming vicarage, and the parishioners had no idea when the bell would ring for the services as the Vicar had to see to the animals. One evening the Vicar was cleaning his shotgun when his eight year-old son came into the study to say good night. The gun accidentally went off and he shot him. It is his spirit that our daughter had seen. We said that it must have been a girl because of the nightdress she was wearing; however, we were reminded that at the turn of the century boys wore nightdresses to go to bed. These details were confirmed by their daughter, who had also seen it quite a few times.

I also experienced one night a heavy weight pushing me through the bed and making me gasp for breath. Fortunately this happened only once. It was quite a disturbing feeling.

Our grandchildren have since told us that they would not go into certain rooms because of the feeling of a presence there. My husband also experienced the pressure of a small hand on his shoulder during the night. At the time all our children were fast asleep in their beds.

With all this taking place, we nevertheless had twenty-seven happy years living there.

Sharon Davison (nee Cooke)

I first had an idea that the Old Vicarage at Clarborough had a presence when I awoke during one night. My parents must have still been up as the back landing light was still switched on. As I sat up in bed I saw a young figure dressed in a long, white nightdress with a shawl draped loosely around it. The figure was standing at the door threshold and the landing light clearly illuminated the figure and its long, blonde, curly hair. I must have gone back to sleep and didn't think any more of the matter really. I think I may have mentioned it to my parents who immediately dismissed it. It was not until a long while later, during a cocktail party my parents were hosting at the Old Vicarage that an American couple said to me, 'We gather your house is haunted!' My immediate reaction was to speak to my parents. It was then confirmed that in fact the 'presence' was indeed there and what I had seen was our little visitor.

We never felt threatened by it. However, on several occasions while studying in my bedroom at the back of the house, my bedroom door would open with nobody there. My wardrobe doors would also open by themselves. I used to have a mobile gas heater in my bedroom to help heat the room. This was sited next to me whilst I was working on my desk and on occasions there would be a definite chill and then either the bedroom door or wardrobe doors would open.

My parents did not tell me about 'Fred', as we used to call him, as they thought I would be afraid of being in the house. But I can honestly say that 'Fred' was no problem at all.

My husband, who was very sceptical about the spirit world, had an experience that confirmed to him the presence of something in the house. It was one Christmas time and he was alone in the drawing-room. At one end of the room was a large Christmas tree. He felt a chill in the room although he was sitting in front of an open fire, and then he witnessed half of the Christmas tree moving, knocking some baubles onto the floor. He was a firm believer after that incident!

At the end of the rear landing is a bathroom which has a very large floor-to-ceiling mirror fixed to its wall. According to the previous owner's daughter, 'Fred' would appear and disappear through this mirror. We, however, never saw it occur.

Christine Durham (nee Stockdale)
Memories of Clarborough School
My mother completed her entire education at Clarborough School; I, together with my seven siblings, also attended the school, but only for our primary education. In the 1950s you started school on or around your fifth birthday, so I must have become a pupil in March 1954. At that time I had an older brother and sister at the school; a younger sister joined three years later.

The school building comprised a big room (Juniors) and little room (Infants), with a scullery at the rear, and an outside toilet block, cycle shed and coke store. There was a concrete playground and an orchard at the back of the school where we were allowed to play and also on sunny days, took our sketchpads out for drawing lessons and in the Infants' days had story-time under the big tree.

We had two teachers: Mr Jones, who was the head teacher and taught the junior classes, and Mrs Hunter, who lived in Clayworth, and was the Infants' teacher. I believe she joined the staff at the school the year before I did, and remained there for many years until her retirement. Mr Jones lived in Hayton and had identical twin daughters, Margaret and Ann. The Jones girls were in my class and the only way we could tell them apart was that one had a strawberry mark on her leg!

The little room was indeed very small and was heated by an open fire. In the winter months we would all sit around the fire for our story-time and after playtime the fireguard would be covered in gloves and socks, drying out in readiness for home time. I do remember having quiet time in the afternoon when we infants were required to rest our heads on our folded arms on the desk. I am sure not much resting took place, but more whispering and giggling.

Perhaps it was supposed to be a quiet time for the teacher, who had to look after and teach all the infant children without any support. We learned to read about the tales of Dick and Dora and their pets Nip and Fluff. Mrs Hunter also taught the junior girls Sewing. We made binca mats, hessian bags and gingham aprons. I even made a rag doll, which I kept for many years.

In the Juniors' (big) room all classes were taught the same subject at one time. At the start of the school day we would have Assembly followed by Times Tables. Our Arithmetic exercise books had squared paper and on the back cover there were lots of useful facts about weights and measures.

The school day ended with all pupils standing – hands together and eyes closed – as we said the Lord's Prayer, before dashing off home down the school hill.

One highlight of the week for me was listening to the wireless. I remember two particular programmes – *Singing Together* and *Rhythm and Melody*. We would sing along with the 'teacher' on the wireless as we learnt traditional songs. The wireless had a very large wooden speaker. The programme that preceded broadcasting for schools was *Desert Island Discs*, and I can remember enjoying the occasions when the wireless was switched on too early and we would catch the signature tune from the previous programme, which is still broadcast on Radio 4.

Our Physical Education lessons were in the big room in wet weather and rounders or stoop-ball outside on fine days. The PE equipment included rush mats, beanbags, wooden hoops and the inevitable bats and balls. We also had instructions in country dancing, such as *Strip the Willow* and *The Dashing White Sergeant*.

School dinners were served by two dinner ladies: Mrs Abbott and Mrs Heathershaw. The actual meals were prepared and cooked at another school – I think this was Carr Hill in Retford – and brought to the school by taxi. We ate our meal in part of the big room so had to clear our desks before lunch could be served. Grace was said before the meal. After lunch, playtime was supervised by Mrs Heathershaw; presumably Mrs Abbott had the unenviable task of clearing up the classroom ready for afternoon school.

One feature of being taught in the village school was Nature Walks. We would go along Church Lane and the Baulk and sometimes to the tunnel top (the railway) to look at signs of the changing seasons and collect items for the nature table. I don't recall letters home prior to our walks or extra adult supervision; we just went along in twos following the teacher.

We also had a visit to Carr Hill School to see a theatre company perform. I don't actually remember the performance but do remember being amazed at the size of the school with so many classrooms and a huge hall with a real stage which had proper curtains – it was like going to a theatre, a real treat.

As the church was immediately adjacent to the school, we were not allowed outside if there was a funeral taking place, and playtime would be moved out of respect to the deceased and mourners. You could not see from the classrooms as the windows were very high.

At Christmas there was always a Carol Service / Nativity Play held in the church and also a party in the big classroom. We would play games like pass-the-parcel, musical chairs and oranges-and-lemons. We also enjoyed a visit from Father Christmas, who was usually someone from the village. I can remember seeing through the disguise of Mr. Wardhaugh, who ran the village shop and post office. At around this time we also enjoyed a visit from a local dignitary, Mrs Jeffcock (I think), who sometimes brought apples from her orchard or tangerines for the pupils.

On one occasion the school was flooded by rainwater running through the school building and we pupils were rescued by Mr Fred Cobb with his tractor and trailer.

The journey to and from school was a major part of the day. We would gather together along the way having racing competitions and challenges to see who could/dare jump the dyke in Church Lane. On one occasion my brother became the school hero after saving a girl from drowning when she fell off the wall on the corner of Church Lane into the pond. His fame did not last long as it was soon discovered that the pond was little more than ankle-deep!

During my last year at the school the building was extended with a new classroom for the Infants and the former Infants' room was converted to a cloakroom and inside toilets. The school also acquired a field at the side, which we accessed via a style in the orchard. This meant more space for outdoor games and additional play area at dinnertime.

I thoroughly enjoyed my time at Clarlborough School, and well remember the apprehension I felt at having to leave to go to the Secondary Modern in Retford.

John Goacher and Helen Shaw Browne (nee Goacher)

John and Helen, with their parents and siblings, moved to Whinley's House in March 1953 and John has remained there ever since. The house is a Grade 2 listed building, built in 1770, and owned by Trinity Hospital, Retford, and John and Helen remember difficult times before the house was renovated. There was no heating, no piped water but a pump in the kitchen, no electricity and an earth closet. They recall being able to see daylight through the roof tiles in both kitchen and attic, and could see and feel the snowflakes floating through in bad weather!

The house has many fine features and shows its age, being built with some really old bricks and with some windows blocked up, one assumes, at the time of the window tax. It is three storeys high with a brick cellar and fireplaces in every room. The beams are genuine and at the time of the renovations the beams in the roof were found to be huge trees still in perfect condition and having rotted only at the gutters. When the flagstones were lifted in the kitchen there was bare clay underneath. Helen remarks that it is no wonder that the carpets became damp and rotted. In the living room that was a kitchen there are still the hooks to hang bacon and the row of bells to summon the servants. At one time a bricked-up door was discovered, leading to the attics, which was thought to have led to the servants' quarters and was possibly bricked up to stop the master of the house visiting the servants!

There is also a glass cabinet hosting a two-headed lamb, a Lincoln Longwool, which survived only two hours and belonged to John and Helen's great-grandfather, Richard Aves, who was a shepherd for Clifford Nicholson and then Henry Dudding of Ruby Grange, Lincolnshire, and said to be the best shepherd there for a hundred years.

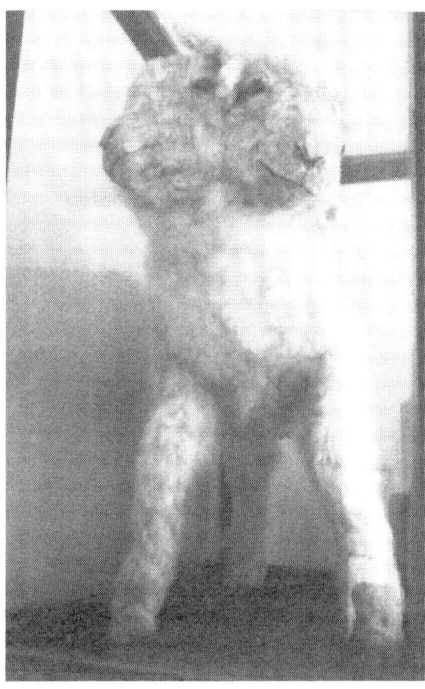

The two-headed lamb

(photo by John Sutton
with kind permission of
John Goacher and
Helen Shaw Browne)

There is also a framed photograph of their father George with the first Charollais bull in the country in the 1960s. George looked after it for a friend; it was evidently a really quiet creature but hugely impressive and strong.

The first Charollais bull in the country with George Goacher
(Reproduced by kind permission of John Goacher and Helen Shaw Browne)

When Verdon Marshall revisited the house he remarked that there was still 'a little Arthur board', which was slotted into the door leading to the kitchen; this stopped Joan's brother Arthur, when young, going into the kitchen, but it had a gap at the bottom of the board to allow the Jack Russell terriers to slide underneath.

As one could expect, there is a ghost story, which revolves round a lady who used to live in Cherry Holt House. The Jacksons, who lived in Whinley's House Farm for sixty years before the Goachers arrived, took her in when her husband died, and some time later she too died. It was exceptionally bad weather and the road at that time was merely a track and they were completely snowed in so there the body lay for a couple of weeks or more. After she was buried she reappeared to haunt the bedroom, where in fact John now sleeps. At the time John's brother Dick mentioned that the room always went cold and then she appeared; then John himself experienced it as a figure at the end of the bed, who once leant over him – at which point he leapt out of bed! She then disappeared through a cupboard at the corner of the room, which was in fact a wig cupboard. On one occasion a certain Doug Stacey, who was a joiner, came to renew a window in the bedroom and was left on his own to get on with the job. He had just broken the old window and got it out when the room went cold, a figure appeared and then went straight out of the window! When the family returned they found a shaken Doug sitting downstairs on the sofa, declaring that he would never enter that room again. The ghost in fact never came back!

Arthur Jackson, son of the previous owners, reputedly would not go into that bedroom, and when the Goachers first entered the house they found the door to this particular bedroom nailed up and the room derelict. Her existence was given extra credence when it was mentioned on one occasion in a letter from Helen's mother to her granddaughter: 'The ghost visited your Uncle John again last night'.

Helen was two when the family moved in and attended Clarborough Village School in 1956. Mrs Hunter was her teacher and Mr Jones, who had twin daughters, was the headmaster. She was able to take a taxi to school until she was seven and then she had to walk. The school taxi was a green Ford Pilot owned by Tommy Parkin from the Hillcrest filling station. Then Mrs Ball from Gringley on the Hill took over. Tommy was very kind and used to pick Helen up, if he was taking another young child to the school, even though he should not have done so as she was older. Sometimes Mr Hall from Sturton High House picked them up and they rode in the back of his van on a bale of hay. This was with Ronald Askew.

On one occasion when Helen, who was a tomboy, was nearly seven, as she waited for her taxi at the end of the school day, she was goading her friends to see how far they could lean over where the sewerage dyke flowed, and of course she was the one who leaned over too far and fell in! Mrs Ball stripped her to her underwear before allowing her into the taxi and, of course, at home it was the tin bath and much scrubbing, particularly as she had on a pot at the time over a broken wrist from falling off her pony.

She remembers crying every morning for six months as she missed the freedom of playing out in the fields, and her teacher remarked to her father that he must have the patience of a saint! She recalls two lovely dinner ladies: a Mrs Abbott who lived on Hayton Smeath and Mrs Heathershaw, who used to live in a cottage opposite Howbeck Lane.

John used to attend Sir Frederick Milner School in Retford and would go on his bicycle, unless it was raining when he would leave it in the wagon shed at a farm on the Main Street nearly opposite Big Lane, where Charlie Jackson lived. In later years Helen also left her bicycle in the wagon shed before catching the bus to school.

The Primitive Methodist Chapel was on the Main Street next to the pavement, where Sunday school and Harvest Festivals were remembered. Helen recalls bidding for harvest produce. When it closed she went to Hayton Chapel next to the Village Hall, which faced the main road.

They both remember the Village Institute, which had a tin roof, lined walls and a wooden floor. It was on Church Lane just after where Rosetta Gleadon's bungalow is now. After the Institute they remember the grassy paddock right up to the dyke and then two cottages where Stanford House is now. Opposite the church were two wooden bungalows, which have now been bricked around. After the church was Church Farm, where Hilda and Harold Bartle lived with their daughter Jillian. They rented the farm from Billy Ward. The orchard had lots of chicken coops. Ken Chapman had more chicken houses further on in a field where the bungalows are now, before the Baulk.

John has happy memories of skating on the pond which used to be at the right-hand corner when facing Church Lane, surrounded by a wall. When the pond flooded and froze the youngsters used to jump over the wall – some of the older ones having visited the Kings Arms first! – and enjoyed their skating.

Up at Whinley's House Farm they were often snowed-in and had a wonderful time sledging on the track, making it as shiny as glass. If they were lucky and got a good speed up they could make it almost to the bottom of the hill. In 1963 the snow was so deep that all you could see were trees – no hedges or vegetation. The bulldozers finally reached them after a fortnight and the snow was piled so high at the side of the track it was still there in May. John described how they had no water as it had all frozen up and they had to go to the Boat Inn at Hayton, and break the water on the canal to take back to the cattle. John went to the village shop on a

Caterpillar tractor. The village fish-and-chip shop was owned by Mrs Bundy, and Granny Cobb, Freddie's mother, used to serve petrol by turning the handle of a petrol pump at a garage next to the Kings Arms.

Judith Gourlay

Judith is a descendant of the Stevensons who lived in Clarborough from the 1830s to 1976. James Stevenson, who married Ann Rogers in 1834, was a carpenter and wheelwright, and they had eight children. The 1851 Census lists James as a publican and wheelwright, and he was living at that time at the Black Woman, just opposite the Kings Arms.

The Black Woman Inn
(reproduced from a postcard with kind permission of Judith Gourley
a copy of this is also in the Bassetlaw Museum)

Of the eight children, George followed his father as a carpenter and wheelwright, as did his son, also a George. James, George's brother, lived next to the joiner's shop on the Main Street. Betsy, the youngest, became a temporary supplementary teacher at Clarborough School, and, as Mrs Hatch, is mentioned several times in the extracts from the school logbook 1910 to 1921, recently reported in the *Retford Times*. She had several absences from school when her husband was wounded and seriously ill and later died, after action in World War 1.

Chapel Row showing the chapel to the left
(Photo reproduced by kind permission of Bassetlaw Museum)

Great Grandad, Charlotte and Lottie on Main Street.

Grandad with Lottie

Grandad with Lottie
(Photos by kind permission of Judith Gourlay)

Clareborough

Parish Magazine.

Price 1½d.   SEPTEMBER, 1923.   Price 1½d.

Vicar—Rev. E: A. PAXTON, M.A., St. Saviour's Vicarage.

Parish Church—

Churchwardens—Messrs. R. E. Clowes and James Stevenson.

Parish Clerk and Sexton—Mr. George Stevenson.

Sidesmen—Messrs. E. Burkitt, A. Gant, S. Oxley, E. B. Seals, A. Tinkler.

Sunday Service—6-30 p.m.   Sunday School—2-15 p.m.

Notices of Baptisms, Banns, Marriages, and Funerals should be given to the Parish Clerk.

St. Saviour's Church—

Churchwardens—Messrs. R. E. Clowes and R. F. Bescoby.

Sidesmen—Messrs. —Chappell, C. Clark, J. Coates, J. Coates (junr.), F. W. Fenwick, P. Fishburne, J. T. M. Gibson, C. Glossop, C. H. Hartmann, Frank Jones, Fred Jones, B. R. Neale, W. A. Paxton, E. S. Pierrepont, J. Richardson, E. Richmond, J. Scoggins, A. Smith, J. E. G. Smith, J. H. Smith.

Organist and Choirmaster—Mr. H. Danby.

Verger—Mr. J. H. Kitchin, School House.

Sunday Services—10-30 a.m. and 6-30 p.m.

Wednesday—7-30 p.m.

Holy Communion—1st Sunday in month at Morning Service ;   2nd and 4th Sundays at 8 a.m. Third Sunday, at Evening Service.

Holy Baptism—Wednesdays, 7 p.m.   Sunday School—9-30 a.m. and 2-30 p.m.

St. Saviour's Mission Room—

Sunday School—2-30 p.m.. Sunday Evening Service—6-30. Thursday—Women's Meeting, 2-30 p.m.

Hon. Treasurer and Secretary for Magazine—Mr. B. R. Neale, 32, Market Square, Retford.

WINTER & SON PRINTERS 24 GROVE STREET RETFORD.

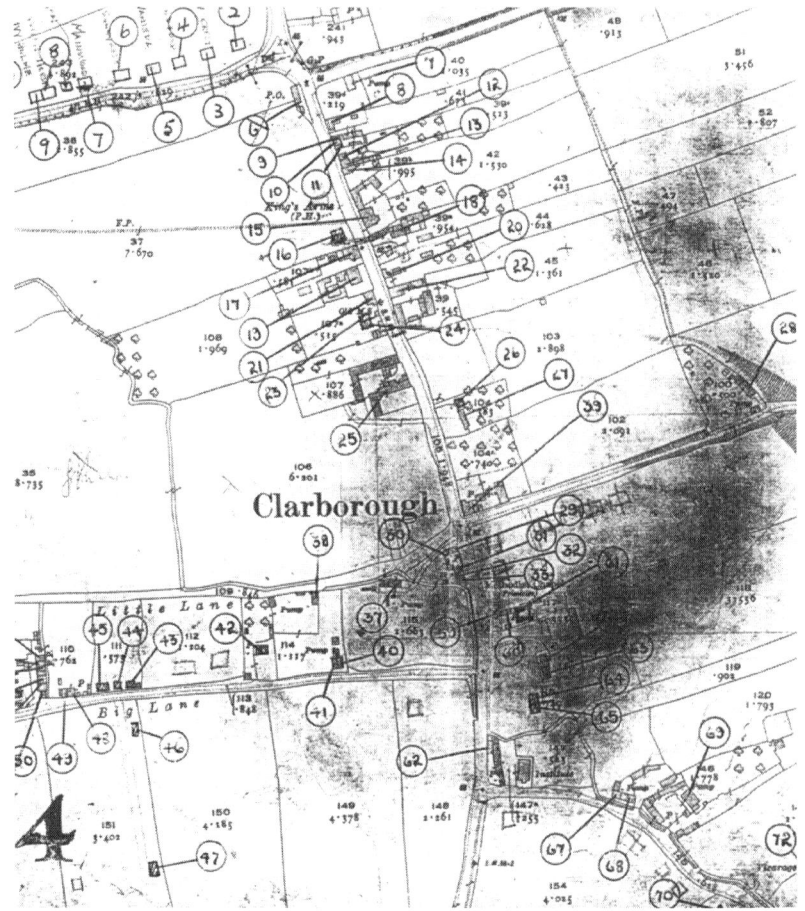

This map shows where Chapel Lane was. Number 28 shows Beehive Cottage at the end of Howbeck Lane

(Map supplied by Judith Gourlay)

Judith's great-grandfather George lived with his wife Kate in Chapel Row, which were two to three cottages lengthways from the Main Street, next to the Chapel. They said when the organ was being played in the Chapel you could hear it through the wall.

His son John, who was killed in World War 1 in 1917, was identified several years later because a part of a postal order, which had been issued at Clarborough in March 1917, was recovered from his body. The postmistress was a distant relative, and knew his family.

George was a wheelwright and also a parish clerk from 1898 to 1935, and also sexton to Clarborough Parish Church from 1894 onwards. Judith has a book in which he kept a record of all baptisms, weddings and funerals in the church, and burials in the new churchyard.

Tom and Charlotte Stevenson are Judith's grandparents, and they lived at Beehive Cottage, Howbeck Lane for some forty years. The house was the furthest up the lane, and until the row of bungalows was built, it was very much on its own. They first lived for a short while in Ordsall, where Lottie, Judith's mother, was born. Then they moved back to Clarborough to a cottage on Main Street before moving to Beehive Cottage.

Tom and Charlotte were both regulars at St John the Baptist church and Tom held the offices of Verger, Sexton, Churchwarden and Treasurer – not all at the same time! And Judith remembers Charlotte going to clean the church.

Judith and her twin sister were born at Clarborough in their grandparents' house and were later baptised at the church. She can remember attending a Flower-and-Egg Festival, and they both had new baskets to bring some of their eggs. She also remembers attending Harvest Festivals on Friday evenings and then attending the Harvest Suppers that followed at the Institute. Her grandparents both died in 1976 and there are now none of her family left in the village.

CLARBOROUGH. — ENTERTAINMENT.
—On new year's night an entertainment consisting of recitations and singing was given in the Primitive Methodist Chapel. Mr. J. Bovill, of Hayton, acted as chairman, and at the close a satisfactory collection was made. Afterwards the children, to the number of 54 received presents from a large Christmas tree, which had been suspended from the roof.

HAYTON.—SINGERS AND RINGEES.—
On Wednesday evening last, the ringers of the Church, and members of the Church choir were entertained to an excellent supper in the schoolroom, Mr. George Smith, churchwarden, and Miss Mee, superintending and looking after the wants of the guests. The children attending the Sunday school also received presents from a handsome Chistmas tree, with which all were delighted.

An extract from the local press, Jan 2nd 1894. It describes some typical entertainment of the time.

Beehive Cottage
(Photo supplied by Judith Gourlay)

Janet Hill

Janet was born in Hayton at Lansdowne House and because of the strong influence of her grandfather, who had become a Primitive Methodist, used to attend the Primitive Methodist Chapel in Clarborough from the age of three years to about ten. She then moved to Welham with her family, first of all to a cottage at the back of Welham Hall, as her father had a job there. Then her father obtained a job in Retford, and they lived in Welham itself.

Janet has very strong memories of attending Sunday school at the chapel and how naughty the boys used to be! The girls were always falling out with the boys and on one occasion a boy hit her on the forehead at which her mother and aunt decided that the boy should be punished. But after much discussion he was let off – except for a warning. At that time parents were much stronger in their use of discipline and often the boys were 'walloped', and of course the cane was used in school.

Janet had a very happy home life but was expected to behave. She remembers the joys of the Saturday penny, which she used to spend on sweets at Mrs Bartrum's farm shop. Great big gobstoppers were not allowed, so she chose jelly babies or hard-boiled sweets at ten for a penny.

Janet and her
sister dressed
for chapel.

A Primitive Chapel outing - by boat to Drakeholes and then on to Pusto
Hill Farm, Everton. This photo was taken sometime before the First World
War   (Photo supplied by W Storrs by kind permission of Janet Hill)

Janet has vivid memories of the annual Chapel Anniversary at which everyone had to say their 'piece', which was chosen by an old lady in Chapel and often was quite unsuitable for their ages, perhaps having to recite Tennyson or Kipling. On one occasion a chosen piece was about death! Her sister had a lovely voice and could reach top G, and was told what to sing with sometimes the choir accompanying her in the chorus. They all had to do what they were told, even the naughty boys! Not all the pieces were well executed, as the shy ones used to speak quickly, gazing up to heaven, and then sit down; but at least, having performed, you could then attend the celebrations. On Sunday they had their anniversary sitting in the choir stalls, and Monday was a day out in the country, after which there was tea in a barn in Clarborough. There was always bread-and-butter to start with (to fill them up), then sandwiches and then the excitement of a trifle topped with hundreds-and-thousands. After that there were games in a field – all well planned and well run.

Janet added, 'A very enjoyable event was when the Sunday school children were taken round the two villages to sing their new children's songs. I remember how very squashed we were in the drays – and how slow the horses were, but perhaps that was because we (all the children) were longing to get back to chapel and our special tea party.'

Sheila and Brian Hogg

Sheila and Brian moved into Meadow Farm in 1958 when it was semi- derelict. There was no damp course and they remember on one occasion distempering the walls of a room one day and waking up in the morning to find it had run down the walls, forming a puddle on the floor! Similarly the previous householders had wallpapered one day and when the wind got up in the night it blew the paper off as the building was only one brick thick. Sheila and Brian also recall one winter evening when the snow had blown under the tiles and landed on the rafters and then onto the ceiling, seeping through and dripping onto them in bed. They had to get a ladder, scoop the snow up in buckets and then pass it down to be thrown out of the window.

This is now the only dairy farm left in the Clarborough and Welham area, whereas when they first moved to Clarborough there were twelve. They described the situation when sometimes the cows would be leaving the farm to go to their fields and would merge with cows from another farm, so one had the worry of trying to differentiate one's own cows and sort them from the group.

Some of the land here is very black and peaty and is very rich for growing; possibly previously it had been a swamp. They remember Mr Tomlinson, a neighbouring market gardener, who still used to use horses to plough. Celery was grown by Mr Tomlinson -– a particular celery called Clayworth Pink. Brian recalls seeing the gardener heaping up the soil at the sides of the celery to cover it and keep it white. Research shows that the *Retford Times* on 7 November 2013 gave details of this celery: 'From the 1870s to the 1950s the celery Clayworth Prize Pink, named after Clayworth, was widely grown on the low-lying soils next to the River Trent which were perfect for celery, a major crop for Gainsborough.

Clayworth Prize Pink won awards in 1947 and 1960 in trials conducted by the Royal Horticultural Society, its leafy stalks described as 'thick, dark pink at base, solid, flavour very good, stored well'. Over the years the number of seed merchants selling Clayworth Prize Pink declined and by 2010 no one was selling seed. So, aware of its local significance, the garden team at Clumber Park started to grow plants in order to produce seeds.'

When Brian was on the Parish Council they were wondering at one time what to call new buildings in the village and he helped choose the name Celery Meadows as being appropriate to the area.

Rhubarb was also grown down the dyke side. There are still hops in the hedgerows and one little field is called the Hop Yard. Another field is called Race Course and was part of the Retford Races Point to Point.

Meadow Farm as it might have looked when originally built in 1777.
(Photo with kind permission of Sheila and Brian Hogg)

They have a photograph, shown here, of the house as it would have been in 1777 when built. Of course, now it has been greatly extended. When they first moved in there was a bread oven on the right-hand side of the house. They had to have the bridge, again built in 1777, strengthened when they stopped using milk churns, as the tankers collecting the milk were so heavy. They had to strengthen it over the top as strengthening underneath would have hampered barges travelling along the canal. Joe Ashton, at that time their MP, helped to advance the proposal.

They remember Harvest Supper in the Village Institute and sitting at Parish Council meetings, hearing the mice rustling and creeping across the beams above their heads. The Institute had a very uneven floor. Sheila has happy memories of her time in the W.I. when a group of them called The Flappers used to entertain and dance. All of their costumes, of course, were handmade. She recalls Mrs Wardhoff, who owned the shop, being the very first Chairman; then Gwen Halford was elected for the second year. Gwen was remembered as being such a lovely and talented lady who used to sew and paint. Brian and Sheila have a beautifully painted picture by Gwen of two shire horses ploughing a field. There were happy memories of Dorothy Burdon belting out *Jerusalem* on the piano at the start of the meeting. The W.I. had a strong choir and Sheila thoroughly enjoyed the practices. She recollects them all having to scrub out the Institute in preparation for their social occasions.

Other memories are of the wheelwright's house opposite the pond and next to the Village Institute at the top of Church Lane. They also remember the filling station on Main Street and how they used to sell tobacco and sweets.

On surveying the land outside the farm Brian mentioned the supposed reason for naming the local lock Whit Sunday Pie Lock.

The strange name reputedly originated when a woman baked a huge pie one Whit Sunday for navvies digging the canal. However, research reveals that recently discovered maps show a local field called Whit Sunday Pie Field that predates the canal.
What a shame!

Ruth Hunter

Ruth describes working at Clarborough County Primary School at the old site from 1953 to 1970. At that time the Juniors and Infants were all on one site and there were approximately thirty children. There was one path to school, near the church, and only one door to enter the school, which was just off the path. The locking of the door was checked every night by the Welham-based police constable with a very large key. Through the school door there were the cloakrooms, the boys on the right, and the girls on the left of the entrance. There was then a door to a large classroom, which was later used as a hall when the school was extended. On the left there were three doors: the middle one led to the Infants' room and the other two doors were store cupboards. The Infants' room was very small – you were only able to walk down the middle of the room. Between September 1953 and January 1954, teachers were not permanent until the new head teacher arrived– a Mr D.L. Jones; then Ruth, the Infants' teacher, was made permanent in February of that year. Mr Jones held a Youth Club on Thursday and Sunday evenings, and the children were encouraged to attend church before the start of the Youth Club session in the school.

At that time a doctor used to come for medicals, which were held behind wooden screens in the large classroom. Ruth remembers one little girl who had to miss much time off school as she contracted salmonella and unfortunately was given negative test results every time she felt she had recovered. Eye tests were also held, and if any defect was found the parents were advised to see an optician.

A Selection of photographs from the
Centenary Celebration 1971

Lady Laycock at Clarborough School

Ruth Hunter, Mrs Pearson, Mr Clark,
Mrs Chambers, Elizabeth Halford

Mr Jones, Mrs Chambers, Ruth Hunter, Mrs Jones, and Mr Clark

Ruth Hunter, Mrs Pearson and Mr Gough

(Photos by kind permission of Ruth Hunter)

There was no central heating, of course, only open fires. A caretaker, Mrs Tunstall, used to leave buckets of coal and everything necessary each morning. There was one large open fire in the large classroom with a fireguard, and at the bottom end of this room there was also a 'Jumbo fire' filled with coal at the top. The base glowed red very often! When the wind was blowing from the north, smoke filled the classroom and the children had to be evacuated until the smoke cleared! There was one large fire with a fireguard in the Infants' (five to seven year-olds) room. In this room there was only the teacher's table and a cupboard. The portable blackboard had to be removed when the children went to the toilet. The desks were wooden with hinged seats for three children and an abacus etched in each place. Ruth was shocked to realise, when she arrived at the school, that the children continued to use chalks, which were coloured and contained in a small tobacco tin with their duster, and they used these with small blackboards.

In the large classroom the children (seven to eleven year-olds) had wooden desks with hinged seats, and the teacher had a high desk. The dinners were brought in containers from Carr Hill School, Retford, and the dinner staff were Mrs B Heathershaw and Mrs Abbott. They served dinners in a space at one end of the large classroom and the children ate dinners at their desks. Dinners cost 9d in old money.

There was no running water for the toilets and they were merely wooden seats with buckets underneath which were emptied once a week. It was discovered that the contents of the emptied buckets were dug into the orchard, and this was a worry because of the children playing there. So from this time they had to be stopped using the orchard. The toilets were outside with one for the staff and three for the children. The washing of hands was done in two water bowls in the small kitchen, which was next to an electric copper used to heat the water to wash the dirty dinner plates, etc. The bowl was on a stool with a hosepipe over a drain which was attached to a tap, and was always slowly filling up and overflowing. There were paper towels for drying hands.

There was no staffroom and space was used next to the coal fire in the large classroom where there was an electric plug. An orange box was used for standing the electric kettle on, with the cups and saucers, sugar, tea, etc in the lower section of the box. There were no easy chairs, so the two members of staff stood up to drink.

The playground was small and children played in the orchard area until the previously mentioned situation arose. Later, part of Mr Bartle's field was made available.

On 19 June 1958 the school experienced water coming down Clarborough Hill because of the really heavy rain, through the orchard area into the small kitchen and then into the large classroom. It eventually came into the new Infants' classroom. The teacher tried to distract the children's attention by singing. Mrs Barthorpe was the caretaker, and she and the head teacher brushed leaves and twigs and water away. Mr F. Cobb, the Chairman of Governors, fetched the dinners from Carr Hill and later transported children and staff to the village in a lorry as the water was so deep. The water was such that it was halfway up the wheels of the lorry. Later, culverts were put in the dyke on Church Lane.

Sports Days were held at Wiseton Hall grounds. This involved other small schools in the area. At Christmas the Infants performed a nativity play in school and later used the church. A Christmas party was held in the new classroom, which has now been demolished, where there were games, and a Father Christmas; Mrs Oxley from Welham visited the school and gave the children

1shilling. (old money), an apple and an orange. This tradition was continued for a time by Mr and Mrs F. Cobb.

In September 1970 the Infants' classes started at the new school in Hillview Crescent; Ruth was deputy head there and stayed until 1990.

On 8 May 1971, when Mr G. Clark was head teacher, there were Centenary Celebrations. The children and staff dressed up in Victorian costumes and the main events were held at the Junior School. Ruth remembers it was a very hot day and all the children's balloons popped because of the heat! The School Queen, Annette Hunt, was crowned by Lady Laycock of Wiseton Hall. There was country dancing, maypole dancing, pony-and-trap rides with Freddie Tomlinson from Cottam, and doughnuts to eat. An exhibition was held in the school.

Mr J Tarr became headmaster in January 1972, at which time the school Chairman was Col. Thomson, ho lived at the old vicarage. Later, Mr F. Cobb became chairman. Mr W. Storrs was Secretary to the Governors, but this task was later taken over by the Education Officer at Retford. Mr Fielding, a later Chairman, frequently visited the Infants' site and always enjoyed tea and biscuits with the staff. He was very friendly. There was no school secretary at first and this task had to be undertaken by the head teacher and his assistant. Girls were taught Needlework and the boys did Craftwork with raffia and clay. There was very little PE equipment, merely ropes, bats and balls.
How times have changed!

Edith Jackson (nee Stockdale)
When I went to Clarborough School there were just two rooms: the Infants' room and the big room. The toilets were outside and there was a scullery with cold water.

On a sunny day we would have story-time under the big tree in the orchard, and we sometimes went for nature walks up the lanes. At playtime we would see a tractor go past to work the field at the top of the churchyard. In winter we would move our desks into a semicircle round the fire and take turns to sit on the front row. Our milk would have ice on the top of it. At Christmas Mrs Oxley from Welham Park would bring us a sixpence and an orange. Father Christmas came to the party with presents for all of us.

My brothers and other older boys would be asked to go pump the organ if there was a funeral at church. They would take it in turns to go, and were paid to pump it with half a crown (today 12 1/2 pence).

We went to Sunday school on the Monday at dinnertime if we hadn't been on the Sunday. When it was the flower service at church we would decorate our baskets in which we placed eggs. There was a Sunday school trip in the summer to the seaside.

We also attended the GFS (Girls' Friendly Society), which was run by Mrs Martin, the vicar's mother, and Mrs Chapman, Ken Chapman's mother. The boys went to Cubs and Scouts.

Mrs Martin paid for Miss Stafford to teach us embroidery. We went to the Youth Club and Whist Drives and dances at the Village Institute. On New Year's Eve we would break at 11.45 pm and go to Church for a short service and to ring in the New Year.

The centre pages of the programme for the Clarborough School Centenary
(kindly provided by Edith Jackson)

When the school was a hundred years old, Susan, Kathy and Stuart were there. They had a May Queen and Maypole dancing. Kathy remembers that they got an orange and a shilling (or, later, five new pence), at Christmas which was now brought by Mrs Cobb. She said they went to Pathfinders and she says she will never forget the white blancmange at Sunday School parties.

Joan and Verdon Marshall

At the age of seven, Joan went to live at Whinley's House, Church Lane, which was her father's family home. Her father had lived there with his parents and siblings since he was six months old. Arthur and Annie, her parents, then went to live in Celery Cottage where Arthur died in 1960. She explained the meaning of Whinley's: 'whin' means gorse and 'leys' means fields – hence a field of gorse, which in fact was what the field opposite was full of until Italian prisoners of war cleared it and chopped all the gorse away.

When she was young Church Lane was very quiet, there being only about five houses which she cycled past every weekday on the way to the Wesleyan School, Grove Street. It was at school that she first met Verdon, although it would be much later that their friendship developed.

She described where the Institute was at the end of Church Lane, next to the Main Road, and how next to it was the blacksmith's, then a field, then a row of cottages end onto the main road. The first of these cottages used to sell small bottles of pop and cigarettes. Then there was the chapel. Behind all these and down Church Lane were many fields. There were also railings, some of which remain today, along from the end of the Institute all the way to the corner where Church Lane bends to the left.

At that time the geographical area of Clarborough extended further than it does now, and she remembers the Clarborough Workhouse being at the top of Spital Hill. The destitute, often soldiers from the First World War, would queue up at night ready for a meal and a bed, for which they had to do jobs. One of them, said Verdon, was chopping up old railway sleepers for firewood, which they then

Some Account of the Trial, Confession, and Execution of

JOHN HEMPSTOCK,

Otherwise Black,

Who was Executed on Nottingham Gallows, on Thursday, March 23rd, 1815,

FOR THE

Wilful Murder of James Snell,

Of Wellam Whinleys, near Clarborough, in the County of Nottingham, on the 5th of November, 1814.

MURDER however, recently it may be perpetrated, can seldom or ever escape the hand of justice; Providence, from whom nothing can be hid, will sooner or later, develope the foul crime,—The unfortunate young man, who has this day suffered the sentence of the law, for a crime the most heinous in the sight of God and man, was born of poor but honest parents, in the parish of West Retford, in the county of Nottingham; of his early habits in life little is known, suffice it, he appears to have been destitute of even the common rudiments of knowledge, so necessary to form an useful member of society. His parents are both dead, consequently have not to witness the agonizing sight of a child perishing by the hands of the common executioner, for a crime the most diabolical in the annals of human depravity.

JOHN HEMPSTOCK was indited (on Tuesday, March 21, 1815,) for the wilful Murder of James Snell, of the parish of Clarborough, Nottinghamshire, on the 5th of November, 1814, by cutting his throat with a razor from ear to ear, and otherwise wounding and bruising him. It appeared in evidence, that James Snell was the nephew of Mr. and Mrs. Wells, of Clarborough, with whom he resided, who left him in the house on the above day, to take care of the same, while they went to Retford Statutes. On their return, at an early hour in the evening, they found their unfortunate nephew weltering in his blood, and a desk belonging to Mr. Wells opened by force, and two bad notes of the Retford Old Bank stolen thereout. It appeared that the prisoner had recently been in the service of Mr. Wells, and on that day he attended Retford Statutes, and purchased two pair of worsted stockings, for payment of which, he tendered one of these notes, and received the change: he also purchased another pair, for which he offered the other note in payment, which was also changed, and he received the difference. The intelligence of the murder and robbery soon began to spread, which coming to the ears of the person with whom he sold the stockings, he was induced to examine the notes he had taken in payment, when it appeared they were the two bad notes which were missing. This soon led to apprehension of the prisoner; and the evidence which was adduced by all the witnesses was so clear, that not a shadow of a doubt remained on the minds of the jury that he was guilty of the murder, and they found their verdict accordingly. The prisoner in his defence, said, he did not commit the murder, but was present when it was done.

The learned Judge on pronouncing the sentence of the law, addressed the unhappy prisoner in nearly the following words,—" John Hempstock, otherwise Black, you have been tried by the laws of your country, and found guilty of one of the foulest offences which can possibly can be committed—the crime of murder ;—a crime obnoxious to the purity of an All-wise Creator, he hath declared that " whosoever sheddeth man's blood, by man shall his blood be shed,"—you cannot deny, but that you have had a fair, candid, and impartial trial, and the evidence produced, cannot leave a doubt on the minds of any one who heard the trial, that you are the guilty person who committed the horrid deed.—You are now in health and the vigour of life and might, by following a regular course of life, have become an useful member of society.—I trust your dreadful example will be a warning to all.—Let me earnestly advise you to make the best use of the short time you are allotted in this world, you must soon appear at the bar of an offended God,—you must shortly pass from time to eternity.—Death is awful even to the best of men,—how awful must it be to you who have so grossly offended against your God. Let me entreat you by penitence and contrition to endeavour to make your peace in this world.—The sentence of the law is, " That you be taken from this place to the prison from whence you came, and on Thursday next, be conveyed to the place of execution, where you are to be hanged by the neck surgeons to be dissected and anatomized ; and may God have mercy upon your soul."

The Prisoner appeared much affected at this solemn juncture, and with tears in his eyes implored one favour from the judge, " that his body might not be dissected, but given to his friend, for burial." The learned judge told him " that favor was not in his power to grant,—the law demanded the sentence should be put in force,—in your awful situation your thoughts should be fixed on better things than what concerns your body, you shou'd think of your immortal soul." The prisoner was conveyed from the bar deeply affected, but on his removal to the prison, he broke out into the most horrid exclamations against the judge, and all the witnesses, swearing that he was an innocent man.

The first time during his confinement that he showed any symptoms of the power of religion on his mind was on the 26th of February, when the chaplain, the Rev. R. Woods, D. D. delivered a discorse from Genesis 42, 21. On the Tuesday following, he sent and desired to speak with him. At that time he denied having perpetrated the murder, but confessed he was privy to it, and he entertained no doubt but he should suffer. The chaplain has been unremitting in his attendance on him, and he has repeatedly declared, that he is not the actual murderer. He seems penitent, He has seen his brother, and the other felon prisoners. He was much affected after his brother left him, and not been able to articulate when he was admitted to the prisoners, the chaplain addressed them in a few words for him.

Bad company has been his ruin. He forgives all who have injured him, and hopes for forgiveness. His whole confidence and trust is in God, thro' the mercies of Jesus Christ. Is reconciled to his fate, and acknowledges the justice of his sentence.

At an early hour on Thursday morning, his irons were knocked off, soon after which he was put into the cart, and conveyed to the place of execution, attended by a great concourse of spectators, and after a short period spent in devotion, he was launched into a never-ending eternity.

HUDSON, PRINTER, RETFORD.

An extract by Hudson, printer of Retford. Kindly provided by Verdon Marshall took round to the local shops to sell. It was evidently a common sight down Carolgate to see a bunch of ex-soldiers, singing away, perhaps with an accordion, their hands outstretched ready, hoping for the odd coin. In the morning one could see a bunch of these soldiers walking from Retford through Welham and Clarborough to Gainsborough to the next workhouse. Of course, some people were residents in the workhouse and one market trader told us about the workhouse penny which was given to them for doing jobs and which they could then spend in the local shops. Before Verdon went into the army he was a telegraph boy and often had to deliver telegrams to the workhouse; he remembers an elderly gentleman who always seemed to be sitting outside and to whom he gave the telegrams.

The Village Institute was the hub of all village events and the village was a really quiet area. All weddings, funerals, and Christmas parties were held there, and both Joan and Verdon enjoyed the village dances which were held every two weeks or so. Joan sometimes went with her uncle, who was thirteen years older. The music was provided either by a piano or by a gramophone, and the events were always well supported with villagers from the surrounding areas coming along. It remained popular until the new Village Hall was built. Verdon remembers some lively times and in particular one young fellow entertaining them all by doing cartwheels down the length of the room!

I asked about the racecourse which had been mentioned, and Joan said that one way to it was down Bone Mill Lane, or alternately from Bigsby Road. People came to the races from all over the country. Verdon remembers that Bone Mill Lane was so named because bones were delivered by canal and were ground down in a building just before the bridge.

Hop-growing was of course prevalent at one time in the area and Joan mentioned that you can still see evidence of hops growing in the hedgerows. Joan moved in 1945 to a cottage down Church Lane where Stanford House now stands, which was one cottage divided into two and was one room up and one down. Carolyn, (Verdon's daughter) and Joan, remember the move from Whinley's, when Carolyn was transported in a home-made bogey, up and down the lane to the new cottage. She described the layout of the cottage with the one downstairs room housing the pantry, sink and fireplace, and from the porch some stairs leading to the one bedroom; she had her bed at the top of the stairs facing the front window with a rail there to prevent her from falling. Her parents' bed was across the room.

Carolyn remembers attending the Clarborough village school from 1947 to 1949 under a Miss Midwinter as her Infants' teacher. She remembers the Christmas of 1948 when the children made ornaments for the artificial tree which were made of cork with pins sticking in the top around which the children wound wool and then made a handle by which they were hung. There were real candles on the tree, as was common at that time, but in fact the tree caught fire and all the ornaments were burnt!

This led to reminiscences about other pupils and she mentions at that time there being three boys with the name John Cobb: John (and Lewis) who were Rosetta's brothers John Cobb who lived opposite the school, and one who was nicknamed 'Johnny whip top'. Everyone had a nickname! She remembers at the end of the Second World War being taken in a Cobb's trailer and tractor with other people into Retford to celebrate.

Joan remembers the land mine going off in 1942 near Whinley's. It is thought that the Germans followed a train from the coast and when it went into the Tunnel they thought it had entered the station and so sent a landmine down on a parachute. It demolished a cottage and broke glass at Whinley's.

The Black Woman Inn on the High Street was owned by a relative of Joan's and, of course, in those days all beer was housed in the cellar and there were no pumps. So the lady who served the beer – Mrs Sprigg –had to walk down the steps to the cellar with a jug each time she needed to replenish, and one day there was a nasty accident when she fell down with her jug. Later, the same building became a fish-and-chip shop.

Verdon remembers the malt kilns at Leverton Road and Thrumpton, and watching barley being spread on perforated tiles under which was the heat; men used to rake the barley wearing canvas boots.

Joan mentioned a murder which was committed at Wellam Whinleys near Clarborough many years previously, and later Verdon gave us a copy of an account of a murder committed in November 1814 at 'Wellam Whinley's near Clarborough'. Evidently a certain John Hempstock, otherwise Black, had been in the service of Mr Wells, the owner of Whinley's and on 5 November 1814, while Mr and Mrs Wells were at the 'Retford statutes', he entered the house, which had been left in the care of the Wells's nephew, James Snell, and 'cut his throat with a razor from ear to ear and otherwise wounding and bruising him'. He then broke into Mr Wells's desk, took notes of the Retford Old Bank and then spent them on two pairs of worsted stockings in Retford. When news of the crime spread, this purchase led to his downfall as the person who sold the stockings examined the two notes and they were found to be the stolen ones. John Hempstock always stated that he had not committed the murder, although was present when it was done.

The learned Judge pronounced the sentence 'That you be taken from this place to the prison from whence you came, and on Thursday next, be conveyed to the place of execution, where you are to be hanged by the neck until you are dead and then given to the surgeons to be dissected and anatomised and may God have mercy upon your soul'. The prisoner was 'much affected', and pleaded that his body might not be dissected but given to his friend, but the Judge said that that favour was not in his power to grant.

So he was imprisoned, declaring his innocence and finally turning to religion. Finally, 'at an early hour on Thursday morning his irons were knocked off, soon after which he was put into the cart, and conveyed to the place of execution, attended by a great concourse of spectators, and after a short period spent in devotion, he was launched into a never- ending eternity'. This was on the Nottingham gallows on Thursday, 23 March, 1815. Reference extract by Hudson, printer of Retford

And this happened in our quiet village!

Jill Palfreman (nee Bartle)

Harold, Jill's father, came to live in Clarborough in 1933 when he was twelve. He moved with his family from Caistor in Lincolnshire to live at South View Farm, Main Street, and then came to Church Farm after his marriage in 1948, later moving to Church Lane Farm when Jill was ten. Church Lane Farm before this was used for housing farm workers.

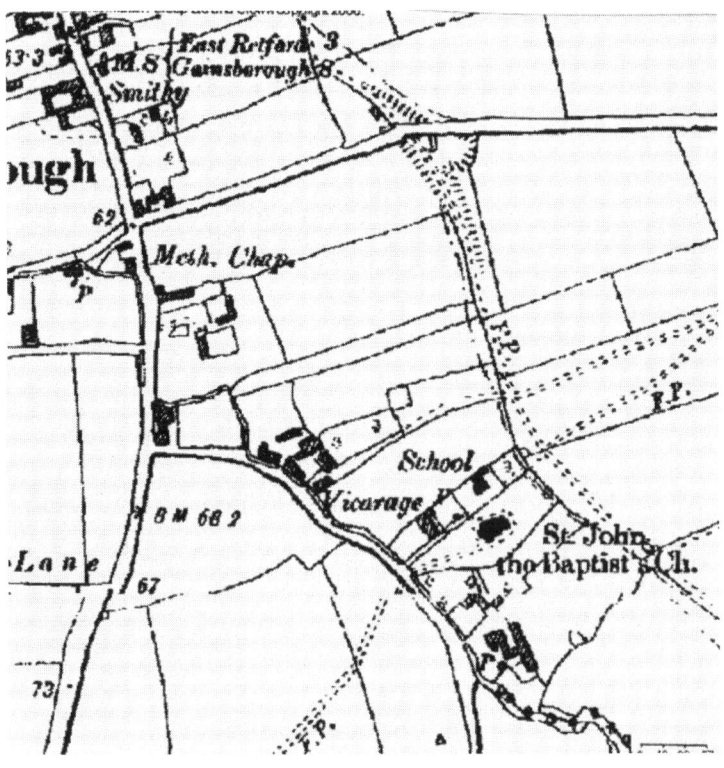

Historical map showing Church Lane Farm,(near the church)
from Chapman's Map of Nottinghamshire 1774.
(Image supplied by Jill Palfreman)

Planked timber door giving access to the roof space and an inscription into the brick chimney breast showing the initials CB and dated 1877

It is the Church Lane Farm which is of great interest as Jill thinks that it is one of the oldest buildings in Clarborough. Certainly on the 1778 Inclosure Map there is a residence on the same site. Research has established that the building has 'significant remains of timber framing', which date it to mediaeval times and is very rare in Bassetlaw. These timber-framed buildings became unfashionable by the late eighteenth century; in fact it had become fashionable after the Fire of London to use bricks.

Beamed internal wall between bedrooms 1 and 2 with brace.

Uncovered, turned balusters which could date from 18th century

(Photos by kind permission of Jill Palfreman)

When Church Lane Farm was altered, the timber frame was encased by bricks. The vertical sliding sash windows, which still remain, have large panes of glass and horn and are thought to be of Victorian design. Indeed, when you look through the trapdoor to the loft, the chimney has 1877 written into the mortar on top of the bricks. A painting dated 1919 shows alterations which have been made since then. (see opposite)

Left: Exposed timbers to the ceiling, showing its age.
Right: Large beam to the end wall (side elevation) of the house.

Roofspace with modern timbers and remains of previous roof
structure visible, which is thought to be of the 1600s
(Photos by kind permission of Jill Palfreman)

When the property was restored in 2005 there was the evidence of its history as when the plasterboard was stripped it revealed the timber-framed internal partitions. When they exposed the balusters of the stairs, before they were enclosed again, these were thought to be 18th century. Whilst the renovations were in progress Jill was visited by a gentleman from Newark who declared that he had traced his family tree back to this house and back to the 1700s. He also mentioned that in his research a 'blue room', which Jill later uncovered, had been used as a Quaker meeting house.

Watercolour painting of Church Lane Farm 1919 (artist unknown)

When the rooms are analysed there are further examples of its historic past. There is a cruck beam in the wall of the small bedroom which also dates the house. Also, the house roof was built on a wooden frame and when the gable was knocked off, there was wood left in the main roof which was thought to be from the 1600s; it remains there to this day. When the ceiling was taken down it was all reeds and wattle and daub underneath and Jill has kept an example of this. The old trapdoor on the landing has an iron hook which is thought to be very old. More studies of this building would prove fascinating.

Ray Pask

Ray was born in Sutton, and then, aged five, moved to Tiln. He schooled at Hayton aged nine, and finally moved to a cottage at Church Farm in the 1940s where his family worked for Billy Ward. Jack Storrs worked there and also John, his brother.

At that time there were few houses down Church Lane. There were the two cottages (now Stanford House), Church Lane Farm, two bungalows opposite the church, the Old Vicarage and Church Farm. A Mr Hill used to live at Church Lane Farm; he later moved to part of Welham Hall. Then Harold Godfrey moved there, before Jill Palfreman's family. Harold Godfrey then went to live past Church Lane corner, in a bungalow which was built as a smallholding.

Ray remembers his Dad working at the Quarry for Billy Ward, looking after the pigs, which used to be next to the Quarry. Billy Ward built Belton House. He remembers Mrs Thorlby, who used to live at the bungalow opposite the wood He also remembers the Hewitts who lived at the crossing house at the side of the track which has now been knocked down. At the cottages at one time lived the Grants, Jack Bannister and Vin Cantrill.

He remembers being a Scout, and attending the weekly meetings run by Billy Ward at the Village Institute. Here there used to be a Friday whist drive and dance. Ray recollects the wooden interior and the tin sheets outside.

Ray's brother John was involved in, and helped to sort out, the sad incident when Mr Briggs's brother-in-law committed suicide in the shed belonging to one of the bungalows opposite the church down

Church Lane. The bungalows, built later on the right-hand side, after the Church, were built by the Cobb family.

Ray recalled with pleasure the fish-and-chip shop in the village, which was open every night. He used to buy his chips and then sit on the wall to eat them. Evidently there was also a fish-and-chip van from Worksop, which used to come round the villages on a Thursday night. The fish-and- chip shop was remembered as being down steps to enter, and then a mirrored image of lovely glass doors, which looked through into the house. The young men also used to visit the Kings Arms and one of Ray's friends used to leave his work at the farm at 10 am, then go to the Kings Arms and buy some eggs, then crack the eggs in his beer, stick a pencil in the yolk to mix it, drink it, and return to his work at 2.30 pm!

Cade's Poultry Farm used to be where the Village Hall is now. Next to the old Post Office there was a farm run by Mr Parkin before he moved to a garage at the top of the hill. Then there was the fish-and-chip shop. Before it sold chips it was two shops run by Mrs Hird where sweets and pop were sold.

Ray recalls the dangerous corner at the bottom of the hill and vividly remembers seeing a cement lorry lying on its side after an accident. He remembers the joiner's shop run by the Stevensons, and the cottage where Mr Boothby and Mr Dunstan used to live.

He used to travel between Church Farm and South View Farm in his work, and remembers one occasion when Church Lane flooded and he was waist-high in water in Church Lane Farm yard with Jill Palfreman's grandfather struggling in the water. He also remembers a fire at Church Farm when the threshing drum was burnt and they sorted out the best of the burnt corn to feed to the hens.

Ray was an active youth and he used to take part in the Boxing Day football match between Hayton and Clarborough in the field in front of South View Farm. He also played cricket in the second field over the Gate Inn Bridge when it was again Hayton versus Clarborough. He also, on occasions, played for the Gate Inn team. There were many friendly matches.

The youngsters at the time were 'sorted out' by the village 'bobby', and Ray remembers Mr Exstall, who lived at the Welham Police House, which was the second house past the bungalows after the bridge. There was then a 'bobby' from Wales, of necessity called Taffy, who used to play cricket with them.

Evidently during the Second World War there were five or six 'look-out' posts fenced off in a field called Top Roughs on the left of Whinley's, up Church Lane. Kevin Booth, who managed to get a look inside, used to say there were beds there.

Freda Robinson
Memories of School Days
In the late 1880s the Jones family came to live at Corner Farm, Welham. This property was demolished in the 1920s and replaced by semi-detached houses, still in existence.
Charles Jones had been a professional huntsman until an accident in the hunting field forced him to leave the hunting scene and take up farming in Welham. He had a sizeable family and the younger children attended Clarborough School. All of the family were regular attenders at the village church.

My father, Percy Jones, seems to have thoroughly enjoyed his time at the school. From the stories he and his siblings recounted, I wonder how much work they actually put in. Schooldays were enjoyed despite the 'stick' applied to their anatomy on occasions, no doubt well deserved. Friendships were made and lasted a lifetime, long after the children had left school to take up employment further afield.

The boys all seem to have known each other by nicknames like Dubber Hebdin, Pummy, Ogle and Kruger Storrs. School meals were not provided and as quite a few children came from distant farms, they had to bring packed lunches. The lunch hour and playtime was the time when mischief and activities took place. Raiding nearby orchards – known as 'scrumping' – was a very popular activity at the appropriate time of year. The boys knew which orchards had the best apples: Russets, Blenheims, Codlings, Ribston Pippins and Beauty of Bath. Some varieties, sadly, are often no longer available. A less popular chore was assisting the 'middenmen' who came on weekly visits to empty the earth closets at the back of the school.

Regular attendance at church was expected at this time, and there was quite a large choir, no doubt recruited from the school. One of the highlights of the year was the choir trip to the seaside. This was long before holidays-with-pay came into force and for many of these children it was perhaps their only excursion of the year.

Pocket-money was scarce and had to be earned. The vicar at this time was, sadly, losing his eyesight. He had asked the headmistress of the school, a Mrs Seal, to send a boy to the vicarage on a daily basis to read the Bible to him. Percy was chosen and was quite pleased to earn a few coppers weekly. He was not so pleased, however, when his mother made him share his earnings with his older sister, who had to stay and escort him home to Welham. One evening Percy, coming to the end of the Book of Isaiah, announced to the vicar that he was now about to start reading from the Book of Jeremiah. On being told to proceed forthwith, he did, and promptly told the vicar and his housekeeper that, at home at Corner Farm, they called their bedroom chamber pot 'the Jeremiah'. On arriving back home sister Connie made haste to report to their parents this embarrassing statement of fact. Percy was chastised and 'grounded', as our children now say, for some period of time. Many years later Grandad Charlie took great delight in recounting the story to his grandchildren.

Another source of income was a regular Saturday job. It was to collect from the local pub in Clarborough, and escort home to Pinfold Cottage in Welham, a gentleman who had only one leg. He was perhaps rather cruelly known locally as 'Pegleg'. After a few drinks this gentleman was not always able to manage his wheelchair, and Frank and Percy were duly employed as escorts. On this particular occasion they found 'Pegleg' in quite a state, and was very difficult to manage into his chair. The boys struggled to get him up the hill towards home, and by the time they'd reached Bone Mill Lane junction, they decided that 'enough was enough'. A strong push sent the chair and occupant whizzing down the hill towards the railway bridge. On reaching the bottom of the hill the chair up-tipped and deposited poor 'Pegleg' into the ditch. They managed to get him back into his chair and eventually deliver him home to his sister's cottage. He was so drunk that he later had little or no recollection of the occasion! 'Pegleg's' nephew, Kruger, was a lifelong friend of Percy, and they often got together in later life and laughed and joked about this incident.

Frank and Fred also had a 'secret' job, in which, had their parents known what the job entailed, they would have forbidden any participation. A lady who lived at Welham Villa was very partial to a glass, or two, of gin. Her family did not approve of this habit, so she had to arrange outside help in obtaining supplies. The wage was 6d per trip (a lot of money for children in those days) for safe delivery of a bottle of draught gin from the Hop Pole Pub. Unfortunately one day, Frank tripped and spilt a small but noticeable amount of this liquor. Undismayed, the brothers topped up the bottle with some disgusting liquid and delivered it to the lady. She did not seem to notice any difference in the taste. The job continued until their parents discovered the subterfuge, and thereupon banned further expeditions to the Hop Pole. So much for selling alcohol to underage customers!

Percy was easily bored with repetitive lessons and was often disruptive in class – hence the 'stick'. However, his classwork was good and he was an avid reader of any book that came his way. It was still in the time of 'Payment by Results' for the school staff, and when the Annual Government Inspectors came round to check on schoolwork, and orally question the pupils, apparently Percy excelled. This seemingly proved that the pupils had been taught, and the staff presumably received their salaries. Mrs Seal rewarded Percy with a florin (ten pence today), which was much appreciated.

Not long before Percy died in 1967, he came out from Retford on his bicycle to visit Clarborough churchyard and the family graves. He was upset to find that the grave of Mrs Seal, his late head teacher, was in a very overgrown and neglected state. He thereupon cycled back to Welham from where he collected buckets, brushes and shears and returned to Clarborough to tidy up her grave. He told his family that Mrs Seal had been strict but fair, and had instilled in him the love of reading and learning, which had never left him throughout his life. He felt that tidying the grave was a penance for his mischief and disruption in school, but also a posthumous thank-you for her constant encouragement.

Joan Tacy

My family moved to a cottage at Sturton High House Farm from Tiln in 1922 and stayed there until Mr Hall retired in 1968. When my family moved in the month of May there was very heavy snow, and potatoes were being planted. Mr Temperton owned the farm then and he said to my mother, 'You know you are nearer to Heaven up here than you are down there!'

Mrs Tacy's mother's cottage (now demolished) at Sturton High House Farm
(photo by kind permission of Linda Lane)

I was one of a family of nine children. I had six sisters, Kathleen, Ada, Annie, Nellie, Joyce and Grace, and two brothers, Alf and Eddie. I was the youngest, born in 1928. We lived in a three-bedroom cottage which has now been knocked down. My father was foreman on the farm and my brother Eddie worked there as well. My husband Arthur Tacy worked there too; that's how we met. We also lived in a cottage at Sturton High House Farm when we married in 1951.

When I was young we used to bike to the dance at the Institute with Marjorie Grant. She lived in the cottages near the crossing. I left her at the bottom of the hill where she lived and I had to walk and push my bike back up the hills home. Lots of people came from other places to the dance and we had some really good dances there. We also had whist drives and musical games in the Institute; we called them 'social evenings'.

Ada Cook is on 2nd row, 3rd from the left.
Alf is on the front row, 6th from left.

Joyce and Grace in their
Land Army uniforms

I attended Clarborough School and started in September although I wasn't five till October. I had to walk two and a half miles there and two and half miles back. Mrs Stevenson was the teacher and she made us march round clapping our hands to warm up. There were forty to fifty children in the school. We had to carry gas masks with us during the war. If there was an air raid we had to go into Clarborough Church. Mrs Oxley brought cake to school for us at Easter. She lived at Welham Park.

Mrs Tacy's brother, Alf, working at Sturton High House Farm
(photo by kind permission of Linda Lane)

We went to the Methodist Chapel on Main Street, Clarborough. At the Chapel Anniversary on Whit Sunday we had to recite verses in the afternoon and again at night. We stayed to have tea with Mrs Green in the village so that we didn't have to walk home and back again in between performances. On Whit Monday we went on the floats. There were two horse-drawn floats: one had an organ on it, and we rode on the other. We always had a new dress and hat to wear for this. We went to the Arthurs' house in Welham; it was up a long drive and the children had to get off and push the trailer with the organ on up the drive to help the horse. Marjorie Thornton (née Grant) fell in the water with her new dress on. We went to Clarborough Church when the Chapel closed.

On Saturday afternoons my Dad took the pony and trap into Retford with three ladies – one from each cottage. One child could go but only if we needed new shoes. All sheep were walked to the sheep fair on Retford Common, and the cattle to Retford Cattle market from the farm, by my Dad and my brother Eddie.

I remember two land mines being dropped near the railway tunnel. They shattered windows. The Paynes lived in the crossing house and the Bennetts and Cockertons in the signalman's house, and their houses were damaged too. The Paynes and Bennetts came to live in two empty cottages on the farm after the bombs until their houses were repaired. We then had a taxi to school when the other children were living in the cottages on the farm and I didn't have to walk to school any more. I was eleven when the war started and can remember when Chamberlain announced war.

Ada made her niece, Linda, a lovely dress for the school centenary
(Photo by kind permission of Linda Lane)

Joan's family at a family funeral in 1976
From left to right: Eddie, Annie, Grace, Ada, Nellie,
Kathleen, Joan and Alf,

During the war one of the cottages was empty, and to help out with the harvest we took in three prisoners of war: two Germans and one Italian. They looked after themselves and did their own cooking. In the winter of 1946 to 1947 the snow was very bad and my Dad and brother Eddie had to make a snowplough out of old railway sleepers so that we could get down into Clarborough village. This helped the Jackson family who lived at Whinley's Farm to get into the village as well.

Joan was interviewed by Jill Palfreman
Photographs kindly supplied by Linda Lane

Bibliography

Primary sources of Information
Clarborough and Welham Parish Council Minute Books
Clarborough School Log Books
Clarborough Show Catalogue 1911
Clarborough and Welham Newsletter March 2008
Enclosure Act 1778
Enclosure Map 1778
Eaton Hall College Education Pack
Parish Magazine April 1931
The Retford Wesleyan Methodist Sunday School Centenary Booklet of 1911
Thesis on Recording Historic Buildings, Claire Edson
Various Extracts from the Retford, Newark, Worksop and Gainsborough
Advertiser, Retford Times and Retford and Gainsborough Times

Secondary Sources of Information
Around and About, Harry Foxley
Board of Agriculture 1794 General view of the agriculture of the East Riding
The Book of Retford, James Roffey
British Listed Buildings - English Heritage
Bygone Bassetlaw 1906
The Development of Education in Nottinghamshire 1889 to 1989
The Early Days of Retford Workhouse Dorinda Clark
Early Victorian Schools in North Nottinghamshire, B. J. Biggs 1977
The East Retford National Schools 1813 to 1858, S. H. Milnes
English Small Town Life 1520-1642
Gamston Schooling Past and Present, K. Sutton
History of Retford, Jackson
The History of Retford, J. Piercy
Kelly's Directory 1848
The Kings England Nottinghamshire, Arthur Mee
Living in Old Retford, B. J. Biggs
The Nottinghamshire Village Book Notts Federation W.I.s
Origin of the Anglo-Saxon Race, T. W. Shore
Some Former Hop-Growing Centres, D. C. D.Pocock
The Story of the Baptists in Retford and Gamston 1691 to 1953, J. Hill
Thoroton Society Article by C. H. Bear on Bolbinus
Thoroton Society Parliamentary Land Enclosures in Nottinghamshire 1743-1860
White's Directory 1832, 1853
Wright's Directory 1879